ADOPTION
A Father's Story

MICHAEL G. GARLAND

Adoption
A Father's Story

Copyright © 2016 by Michael G. Garland

ISBN-13: 978-1539168164
ISBN-10: 1539168166

To My Beloved Children,

Anna, Grace, Emma, Wikelson, Daniel, and Richardson:

May you all receive adoption in Christ and the Spirit by

which we call out "Abba! Father!"

(Romans 8:15)

TABLE OF CONTENTS

ADOPTION TIMELINE

Wikelson's birthday	**September 1, 2010**
Richardson's birthday	**August 18, 2012**
Our decision to adopt	**March 2013**
Formal adoption application	**April 23, 2013**
Adoption training complete	**July 5, 2013**
Home study #1	**October 2013**
Wikelson and Richardson arrive at orphanage	**January 20, 2014**
Home study #2	**March 2014**
Home study #3	**April 2015**
"The Call" matching us with the boys	**October 31, 2015**
Socialization visit	**November 19 – December 3, 2015**
Adoption decree	**March 10, 2016**
Passports issued to Wikelson and Richardson Garland	**June 16, 2016**
Final clearance by USCIS	**July 26, 2016**
Arrival home	**August 20, 2016**

ACKNOWLEDGEMENTS

This adoption and therefore this adoption book would never have been possible without the specific and sacrificial intervention of all those named below. In addition to those listed, many others provided an encouraging word, prayed for us, and helped us along the way, and each of you is greatly appreciated as well.

Jon and Barb Parson

Dan and Kathy Garland

Diana Boni

All Blessings International

Toby and Mandy Conklin

Greg Austin

Janna Shearer

Kathy Skinner

Matthew Magana

Eileen Saemenes

Fred and Diana Bradshaw

James Ballard

Fern Campbell

Show Hope

The Staff at BRESMA Guest House and Orphanage

Good Shepherd Community Church

Frances Garland

Many more who prayed for and encouraged us

INTRODUCTION

It ALL BEGAN before the foundation of the world. Before the spoken Word of God commanded the light to break through the darkness, it was there. Before the mountains bathed in the warmth of the very first sunrise, it had started. Before the first eagle soared majestically in flight or the first enormous whale broke powerfully through the waters' surface, it had begun. Before man had drawn his first breath, loved, blessed, hated, or cursed, it was in motion. It was a story—a story envisioned and written before the ages and for the ages. It was God's story, a Father's story, your story, and my story.

At its core the story is about relationship and love, but it is filled with rebellion, brokenness, pain, sacrifice, forgiveness, renewal, redemption, and rewards. It is a great story about a Father calling the fatherless home. It is a story about a love that would go beyond the limits of comprehension to restore that which had been lost. It is a tale like no other, the master Storyteller weaving together each strand of thread into a tapestry so complex and beautiful that it takes a lifetime to understand, and yet so simple that it can warm a child's heart. It is THE STORY in which all other stories find their home, and somewhere hidden deep within its pages, perhaps in one of the lesser-read chapters buried in one of the rarely chosen volumes, is my story. As He has done for all believers, God saw me before time began and chose me to be a part of His wonderful family story. As small and insignificant as I may be, I am humbled to think that God, in this epic narrative, had a special role reserved for me.

The great story is about *the Father*. My story is about *a father*. Both tell of a love for children and the journey undertaken to bring them home. Both are about finding those who were far off, without hope or home, and bringing them near. My story is a dim reflection of the Father's, just a faint glimmer of something more, a sign that points to the actual destination. My story finds its roots as well as its meaning in the Father's story, and it could not exist without Him as the source. In this book I want to share with you my story as a father bringing children home through human adoption, and in doing so, point you to the Story, in which the Father brings His beloved children into His eternal home through redemption and divine adoption.

God loved—and so began His story. Out of the triune, eternal, and loving relationship of the Father, Son, and

Spirit, God created, His love overflowing and bringing forth new life where it had not existed before. God created light, space, time, matter, galaxies, stars, planets, and the earth and everything in it. The wonders of the universe are the handiwork of His fingers, and yet these are not the pinnacle of His creation. All the marvels of the world, no matter how spectacular they may be, were simply prepared as a home for the capstone of creation and object of His love: human beings. Out of all creation, the man Adam and the woman Eve were the only ones to be made in the image of God. God created Adam and Eve *from* an eternally loving relationship and *for* an eternally loving relationship. They were meant to be a part of God's family, enjoying His presence daily as He communed face-to-face with them in the Garden of Eden.

But as we know from reading the book of Genesis, a rebellion entered into the family relationship, causing a wide chasm between Adam and God. The obedience of Adam to his own will rather than to God's resulted in separation, pain, punishment, and death. An estrangement occurred when the man Adam set out to make his spiritual way alone. But fortunately the story did not end there, because God had a plan for redemption and restoration. God did not leave His children without hope, but He told of a promised Savior who would come and set all things right and make all things new. This is the great Story: God, the Creator of the universe and of life itself, left His throne and took on the flesh of a man whom we call Jesus, entered into enemy-held territory, suffered pain and death, and rescued sons and daughters who had gone astray. And there is more. Not only did God rescue those with no hope, but He did so to adopt them into His own household, bestowing upon them all the rights and privileges of being children of the King.

The Father's story is filled with wonderful pictures. Because His story is vast and intricately detailed, we find microcosms—small pictures and themes—that point back to Him as the Author. As you read this book, you will not see any actual pictures, and yet it is full of them. God has designed life in a way that reflects His goodness and glory, and even in these difficult times of sin and separation, His plan for relationship is modeled in our daily lives. One of these pictures is found in adoption. As you read my story, it is my intention that you see it as a reflection of God's story and that you would be drawn to Him as a Father who loves and seeks out spiritual orphans.

A STORY WITH MANY PICTURES

THERE ARE PICTURES all around us. We find them in books and magazines. They hang on the walls of our homes and businesses. Our smartphone storage capacities are stressed to the limit because of them. We create scrapbooks filled with pictures of family, friends, and good times. Walk the busy streets of any downtown and you will find plenty of pictures in the form of advertisements, signs, and murals. They are used in countless formats, from engineering plans to medical imaging to real estate sales. Pictures are so ubiquitous in our culture that it would be difficult getting through twenty-four hours without seeing one.

Why are we so enamored with pictures? Why do we spend so much time and money to make sure that the scrapbooks on our shelves and the walls in our homes are full of them? After all, a picture is not real. It is just an artificial two-dimensional impression of the real thing. With the exception of some forms of modern art, most of our pictures relate to something that actually exists, like a person, place, or event. So why do we focus so much on imitations? I believe that one of the reasons we love them so much is that pictures point us to, or remind us of, those real things. When we are away from a loved one, for example, a picture serves as a kind of reminder that brings back memories that might otherwise fade. A beautiful scenic picture is captivating, but only because it makes us long for something more. Someday I would like to visit the Grand Canyon, not because I have read a book or because I spoke with someone who told me about it, but because I have seen pictures of it. When I see a picture of the Grand Canyon, I am struck by its majestic beauty and I appreciate it, but my feelings don't stop there. Those breathtaking images create in me a desire to see the canyon for myself and experience its grandeur firsthand. The same is true for pictures of family that we place in strategic locations throughout our homes. Of course, these images are not our "real" brothers, sisters, children, or parents, but they serve to stir a memory, invoke a thought, or remind us of someone special. Pictures are valuable because they are arrows that point us to something better. They are signs that point to a destination. They are reminders that there is more to life than our immediate surroundings. Pictures help us to look beyond our current circumstances and think about what was in the past or what will be in the future. They are a fundamental part of the human experience.

Our adoption story led us to Haiti, where two beautiful

boys were waiting for a family. Over the final year of the process, we traveled to Port-au-Prince two times—the first to meet the boys and the second to bring them home. During our initial visit our eyes were drawn to the abundance of artwork present in that culture, and we were happy to have the opportunity to purchase several oil paintings. Carefully removed from their frames, the canvas works of art were rolled neatly and tucked into our suitcases as we brought them home to enjoy. The images included a colorful market scene, two young boys on a fishing boat inscribed with the phrase "Thank you, God," and a sugarcane field. The paintings are lively and colorful, and any casual observer could appreciate them for their aesthetic quality. For us, however, they are much more than just pretty paintings. They serve as a reminder of a time, place, and experience. Once an observer understands the context of the paintings and what they mean to us, there is an added dimension of appreciation that was not present before. When we explain that the two small boys sailing in the fishing boat represent our two adopted sons and the inscription of "Thank you, God" reminds us of our gratitude to God for bringing them to us, the whole image changes. It is transformed from just a nice painting into a meaningful reminder.

God loves pictures. I can say this with confidence because He has filled His Book with them. Over and over in the Old Testament Scriptures, images point to Jesus. From the first coverings God provided for Adam and Eve, to the offering of Isaac by Abraham, to the serpent that Moses "lifted up" in the wilderness, to the blood that covered the doorposts at the Passover, to Jonah's three days in the belly of the great fish, the Bible tells the story of Jesus by using actual historical events as pictures pointing to Him. Pictures are not only prevalent in the Old Testament writings but are found in the New Testament as well. Practical insight for Christian living is found in the picture of the body with its ears, eyes, feet, and hands each representing a different role in the community of believers. Communion is a vivid picture that reminds us that Jesus's body was broken and His blood was spilt on our behalf. Baptism is a representation of the believers' association with Christ in His death, burial, and resurrection.

When He walked on this earth as God incarnate, Jesus taught primarily using word pictures and parables. He used common things to explain profound mysteries. By using simple pictures such as a mustard seed, He was able to reveal profound truth about the kingdom of God. In the Gospel of John, Jesus described Himself as, among other things, the Light of the world, the Bread of life, the True Vine, and the Good Shepherd, all of which are pictures illustrating the nature of Christ. Recently I was browsing the shelves of our church library and I found a "Dictionary of Biblical Imagery" that is a very large book dedicated solely to detail and explain the multitude of pictures found in God's Word. Space prohibits me from detailing each and every one, but I think "you get the picture" that God's Word is full of them.

It is not just the Old Testament stories, New Testament analogies, or the teachings of Jesus, but even the creation itself is a picture that points to God with its incomprehensible size and indescribable beauty. "For what can be known about God is plain to them, because God has shown it to them. For his invisible attributes, namely, his eternal power and divine nature, have been clearly perceived, ever since the creation of the world, in the things that have been made. So they are without excuse" (Romans 1:19-20). And it doesn't stop there. Even today, two thousand years after Jesus walked among us, there remain pictures strategically placed by God to point us toward Him. When we look at life's pictures the way God does, they are transformed into meaningful reminders of the Artist who painted them. We live in an art gallery full of self-portraits of God. Many of these "self- portraits" are found in the way that we relate to one another. That makes sense because God is the Creator of all relationships. In the following sections, we will take a closer look at how the relationships of marriage and parenting image our heavenly Father for the purpose of "priming the pump" before examining adoption in greater detail. It is helpful to understand that adoption, as a picture of God's love, is not unprecedented but rather follows a pattern that God has established from the very beginning of time, in which He uses earthly pictures to point to heavenly realities.

MARRIAGE

"Therefore a man shall leave his father and his mother and hold fast to his wife, and they shall become one flesh" (Genesis 2:24). These words were written regarding the first marriage that God Himself performed when He brought Eve to Adam to be his wife. For hundreds of years, before

Jesus Christ set foot on the earth, and before any of the New Testament books were written, that passage would have been understood by Jewish rabbis as a reference to human marriage. And why wouldn't it be? It seems to be very clearly describing the way that a man would start his own family by leaving his parents and being joined to his wife. But in the New Testament we learn that marriage is a picture of something much greater.

It is true that Genesis 2:24 can help us to understand the marriage relationship between a man and a woman. But in a twist that perhaps even he did not see coming, Paul, inspired by the Holy Spirit, wrote that it was referring not just to human marriage but to Christ and the church. After quoting Genesis 2:24, he wrote, "This mystery is profound, and I am saying that it refers to Christ and the church" (Ephesians 5:32). Paul was teaching that marriage is an important picture reflecting a deeper reality that is Christ and His church. As Christ loved the church and sacrificed Himself for her, so should the husband love his wife sacrificially. As the church submits to the loving leadership of Christ, so should the wife submit to her husband's loving leadership (Ephesians 5:22–25). Paul revealed that marriage, as important as it is in our daily lives, is not an end in itself but rather an example of something that is true about God.

Marriage is also a picture of the nature of God. Trinitarian theology teaches that there is one God that exists in three distinct persons. (See the section on adoption and the Trinity.) Each person—the Father, Son, and Holy Spirit—are equal, but they each have different roles. The marriage relationship images that reality in that the man and woman are equal, but they both have distinct roles. Somehow in a marriage two people become as one person but still retain their unique personalities and roles. This is a mystery, but it is one that the Bible clearly teaches with regard to the "one flesh" nature of marriage and with regard to the Trinitarian nature of God. The "one flesh" relationship is one reason why divorce is so messy. It has been said that divorce does not leave two unbroken pieces, but instead it leaves only one piece that has been broken in two. Both parties are incomplete after divorce because each one has left a part of themselves with the other. If that makes any sense at all, it is because the two had become one—just as God in three persons is one.

In the institution of marriage, God has chosen to paint a picture that reveals to us truths that we otherwise may not be able to grasp. If we look at marriage the way He looks at it, our focus will shift from the picture itself to what the picture actually represents. Looking at marriage without God's perspective is like a stranger in our home looking at our Haitian paintings with no explanation: they are nice, but nothing more. Once we see marriage in its proper context, our eyes are opened and our hearts are drawn to the beauty of the Trinity and the relationship that Christ has with His church. As always, the destination is better than the sign that points toward it.

PARENTING

Our family would not function without Joelle. Her role as a mother is invaluable, and I thank God often that she embraces it with joy. I remember a frank conversation that occurred one day with one of our younger children. One of the best things about kids is that they haven't figured out yet how to pull any punches and so they just say exactly what is on their minds. The child was wondering if it was necessary to love both Mom and Dad the same, saying, "I think I might love Mom a little more." As a father, that did not hurt my feelings at all. In fact, that's the answer that I would expect, because Joelle provides nurturing care in all aspects of their little lives in ways that I could never do. From bathing, to feeding, to teaching, Joelle is always there. The voices she reads in are more fun than mine and she does better tuck-in times for bed that usually involve a sweet song and a spoken blessing. If our home was not filled with the sacrificial love that Joelle shows in meeting the needs of our children, we would never have considered adoption. Her role is absolutely crucial.

Having said all that, as far as pictures are concerned, the Bible never describes God as a mother. God as a parent is never depicted as feminine, but always as the Father. The only exception may be when Jesus said, "How often would I have gathered your children together as a hen gathers her brood under her wings, and you were not willing!" as he mourned over the city of Jerusalem (Matthew 23:37). While it is true that God is called our Father, keep in mind that He created both men and women in His image and He charged both with the role of parenting. I believe that to a certain extent, both a mother and a father as parents are necessary to reflect the Fatherhood of God. God is never out of balance or in tension with Himself. If only males reflected the Fatherhood of God, the picture would be out of balance because it would be lacking all the godly qualities that females bring to parenting. Where do women get their nurturing instincts if not from God? Even though we only have one spiritual parent in heaven, it may take two parents to best picture Him on earth.

With that in mind, the idea that earthly fathers are a picture of the heavenly Father is an obvious connection. In the Sermon on the Mount, Jesus used this picture when He said, "Or which one of you, if his son asks him for bread, will give him a stone? Or if he asks for a fish, will give him a serpent? If you then, who are evil, know how to give good gifts to your children, how much more will your Father who is in heaven give good things to those who ask him!" (Matthew 7:9–10). In other words, if an earthly father who is just a dim reflection of the "real thing" can provide for his children, then how much more will the heavenly Father provide for His? Earthly fathers serve as a very tarnished, but nevertheless, useful picture of God the Father as they try to instruct, correct, discipline, and love their children.

Jesus showed us the original Father/Son relationship that is the basis of all earthly parent/child relationships. His relationship to His Father is the "real thing" that all earthly parental relationships have the potential to reflect. By affectionately calling the Father "Abba" ("Daddy"), submitting to His will, and relying upon His provision, Jesus gave us a perfect example for how Christians should approach God. I have heard it said that the way our human fathers relate to us will dramatically impact the way we relate to the heavenly Father, either for better or for worse. If that is true, what a sober reminder for fathers to model their love and care after the example of God and thereby paint an attractive picture of the heavenly Father with the goal of pointing their children to Him.

Fathers and mothers image God in parenting. That was God's design. When children are raised with the love and discipline of caring parents, it provides a foundation from which they can then relate to their heavenly Father. The sharper the earthly picture, the better it points to the heavenly reality. On the other hand, if the earthly picture is damaged and/or faded, it leaves children without a model of a loving Father in heaven, which can make it more difficult for them to believe in such a God.

ADOPTION

Parents adopting orphans can be viewed as a picture of a loving God bringing spiritually hopeless children into His home at unthinkable cost to Himself. In the remainder of this book, I will be telling my specific adoption story with the purpose of pointing you to God's ultimate adoption story. Before we move on, however, I want to distinguish between intentionally and incidentally imaging God. To be intentional is to do something on purpose for a specific reason. In contrast, an incidental event just happens. It is one thing that occurs while you are doing something else. It is interesting to note that most pictures of God that are found in this life happen incidentally, at least on a human level. Moses had no way to know that when he lifted up the serpent in the wilderness to provide healing for the people who would look up at it, that he was reflecting Jesus Christ as He would be lifted up on the cross centuries later. In the same way, Isaac would have had no idea that his near death upon the altar at the hands of his father Abraham would image Christ's actual death by the hand of His Father. Those were profound pictures of Christ that nobody recognized at the time the events occurred. Of course, God knew what He was doing and whom He was pointing to, but for the people involved, the imaging of Christ happened incidentally. The examples of marriage and parenting for the most part image God incidentally. Nobody decides to get married in order to image Christ and the church, just as no one decides to have children because God is their heavenly Father. Those events happen all the time, and even though they always image God, the participants are often unaware of that fact. Incidental imaging is not a negative thing, and it is different from an accidental occurrence because it does not represent a mistake or a problem; it is just something that is not done on purpose.

That brings us to the intentional imaging of God that is setting about doing some activity for the primary purpose of pointing to God. Adoption is one way that we can intentionally image God. (Other examples include forgiving an undeserving person or loving the "unlovable.") While intentional imaging is not true of every adoption, it is true of many, and with the growing adoption movement seen in our churches today, it is becoming more common. One of my primary motivations for moving forward with our adoption was to intentionally image God. My marriage and my becoming a father both point to God, but these are incidental images—the imaging of God was not my primary motivation for either one. By adopting, however, I wanted to intentionally draw attention to and picture the love that my heavenly Father has lavished upon me (see 1 John 3:1)— and not just draw attention to it, but share it with those who do not know the love of a father. I did not "need" more children. Frankly my life would have been much simpler had we not chosen to adopt, just as it would be simpler if we did not have four biological kids. Our adoption was not meant to complete us or to fill something in us that had been missing before. It was not to fulfill my desires that I chose to adopt. Only God, not anything else in the world, can meet our deepest desires. It was love that motivated me. The same love that had been shown to me was now flowing through me to bless another. In that way, adopting actively painted a picture of God and what He has done in my life by inviting me into His home when I had nothing. On a human level our adoption meets a real need that is a home for orphan children. That motivation in itself is valid; however, how much more profound is the adoption process when seen in terms of the heavenly reality that it pictures.

It is important to understand that intentional imaging as a primary motivation does not diminish the act of adoption. Our adopted sons should never feel slighted that reflecting God motivated me. On the contrary, they should be delighted because the closer I image God as a father, the better I will care for them as sons. To image God and His love is the very best thing I could do for any of my children. Loving my children on a purely horizontal level is good, but how much better is it to model the perfect love of the Father above. The same is true for my marriage. Joelle would not be slighted in the least if I modeled my love for her as Christ loved the church, because the closer I approach that kind of love, the better husband I will be. Christ gave Himself up, being emptied of the glory of heaven, to become a servant who would eventually die because of His love for His bride—the church (see Philippians 2:7–8). If I could be even a faint shadow of that type of love, how much better would my marriage be? If that kind of love was on display in my life, I do not believe that Joelle would criticize me for having a God-centered motivation. Intentionally imaging God, therefore, is not a negative at all, but rather it is the center of the target that Christians should aim for in all their endeavors.

In the next chapter we will spend some time focusing on what the Bible has to say when it comes to the Father's heart for adoption. The truth found in God's Word is what supports and motivates my entire story. I cannot rightly tell that story without first laying out the theological foundation on which it is built. While foundations can sometimes seem uninteresting or dull, they are of vital importance to the integrity of any structure. A house built without one is sure to falter and fail, and I believe wholeheartedly that without God as the foundation of our adoption, it would crumble. So we will start at the beginning—the foundation—and then build upward from there.

THE FATHER'S HEART
FOR ADOPTION

DEFINITION OF TERMS

I WILL ALWAYS REMEMBER the first employee contract I signed. The year was 2003. I had just graduated from the Physician Assistant program at Alderson-Broaddus University in Philippi, West Virginia. Following a long thirty-six months of didactic and clinical training, my degree was complete and I was eligible to sit for the national board exam. Thankfully, because of the thorough preparatory instruction I received, I was able to pass the exam on the first try. Now all I had to do was find a job. After several interviews I was given an opportunity, and being a new unemployed college graduate with a pregnant wife and a young daughter at home, I pounced on it. I was presented with a contract to review, and prior to any details about job-related responsibilities, expectations, conduct, or compensation, I found a "definition of terms" section. At first, this section seemed very unnecessary, as it spelled out with excruciating detail, among other things, what was meant each time the word "employee" was used, making it very clear that it was referring to "Michael Garland" and nobody else. In the same way, the "employer" was delineated very specifically as one in the same with the medical practice whose logo sat atop the letterhead. There was to be no doubt about the seemingly obvious definitions of all the parties, locations, and other details that would be referenced from that point forward in the contract. Although this minutia seemed to be readily evident, it was important to define because in the event of a dispute, no party could claim that they did not understand the terms.

Isn't it true that in many of life's disputes, whether they be political, religious, or personal, there is a lack of a consistent use of terms that are well defined and agreed to by all those involved? In many cases, we just talk past one another because the terms of the argument, the words we use to make our case, are misunderstood. I have come to appreciate the "definition of terms" section in my first contract as well as subsequent contracts because of the clarity it brings to the discussion, even if it seems a little unnecessary at times. Clear definitions lead to clear communication, and that is my objective as I tell this story.

As you read through these pages, the word "adoption" will be used to describe two different events. The first refers to humans adopting humans, otherwise known as "horizontal adoption," and the second refers to God adopting humans, otherwise known as "vertical adoption." Vertical adoption is a two-part process that begins with redemption, the payment of our debts by Christ, and ends with adoption, the making of "sons" for an eternal inheritance of life (there will be more on this later). The subtitle of this book is *A Father's Story* because it is about me as *a father* brining two boys into our family by way of horizontal adoption, but it is also about God *the Father* bringing me, and other believers, into His family by vertical adoption. Just as we love because He first loved us, we adopt because we were first adopted. If we can start with a God-centered view of life, then our perspective on all relationships, including adoption, changes as we discover that He is the source of each one. While there are certainly differences between horizontal adoption and vertical adoption, the common ground that they share is unmistakable. Our attention will be directed toward the relationship between these two wondrous events, with a focus on horizontal adoption as it flows naturally, springing forth from the headwaters of vertical adoption. The fact that God, through the person of Jesus Christ, seeks out and invites the lost into His home is the Gospel message, and what better way to picture that Gospel message on a human level than by horizontal adoption?

Adoption is taking someone who is not a natural-born son or daughter, and by means of a legal transaction, changing his or her status to equal that of a natural-born child. It is the inclusion of one, previously associated with an old family, into a new family. It is the addition of somebody, previously an outsider, into a family relationship.

Most commonly it means taking a child who has no viable parent or home, and giving him both. This legal transaction not only provides the child with parents, but it also bestows upon him all the rights, privileges, and responsibilities of being a member of that family. Here is the question: Did I just describe horizontal adoption or vertical adoption? As we will see, I believe that the answer is both, because horizontal adoption is modeled after vertical adoption, and the similarities are quite striking.

CHILDREN OF WRATH

Adoption always involves children. Both horizontal adoption and vertical adoption share that theme. But how can God, if He is the Creator of all things, adopt children that are already His? Don't all people belong to Him by virtue of the fact that He made them? God, in one sense, is the Father of all people because He created them, but He is the spiritual Father only of those who have been redeemed by a saving faith in His Son Jesus Christ. Jesus can be thought of as the only "natural-born" Son of God. All God's other children become so because of their union with Jesus, which gives them access to the Father. Spiritually speaking, only two kingdoms exist in this world and two fathers that rule over those kingdoms. There is the kingdom of light that is of God and the kingdom of darkness that is of the devil. As hard as it is to accept, the Bible teaches that each person who has ever lived is either a child of God or a child of the devil. Because that appears to be an extreme claim, we will take a moment to look at some examples.

In His explanation of "The Parable of the Weeds," Jesus described two types of people in the world: "The field is the world, and the good seed is the sons of the kingdom. The weeds are the sons of the evil one" (Matthew 13:38). When confronting the Pharisees, Jesus said, "I speak of what I have seen with my Father, and you do what you have heard from your father" (John 8:38). He continued on to show that their father was the devil (John 8:39–47). In his rebuke of Elymas the magician, Paul said to him, "You son of the devil…" (Acts 13:10). Ephesians 2:1–3 describes the prior state of believers as following after the prince of the power of the air (Satan) and as "sons of disobedience" and "children of wrath." In his description of the righteous acts of the children of God, the apostle John said, "By this [the righteous acts] it is evident who are the children of God, and who are the children of the devil" (1 John 3:10). Notice that John only allowed for two categories here: the children of God or the children of the devil. The assumption is that all people fit into one of these two groups. Simply stated, if you are not a child of God, then you belong to the devil.

I have taken the time to cite several passages because the idea that we are the spiritual children of either God or the devil is a hard teaching, but I believe that it is an undeniable reality that Jesus Himself taught—and it is one of the keys to understanding vertical adoption. The fact that, before God adopted us, we were children of the devil is a sobering thought. If not for the redeeming "But God" in Ephesians 2:4, we would be languishing eternally in our hopeless state as "children of wrath" instead of enjoying the riches of being children of God. "But God, being rich in mercy, because of the great love with which He loved us, even when we were dead in our trespasses, made us alive together with Christ" (Ephesians 2:4–5a). By the process of redemption and adoption, God took children who were not naturally His own, and made them His own, granting them access to Him as their Father, and providing them with an eternal inheritance of life. In doing so, He moved them from the kingdom of darkness to the kingdom of light through Jesus the Son. "He has delivered us from the domain of darkness and transferred us to the kingdom of his beloved Son, in whom we have redemption, the forgiveness of sins" (Colossians 1:13–14).

CHILDREN OF GOD

"See what kind of love the Father has given to us, that we should be called children of God; and so we are" (1 John 3:1). In his gospel the apostle John referred to himself several times as the disciple "whom Jesus loved" (see, for example, John 21:7). This was not because he thought of himself more highly than the other disciples, or that he thought Jesus did not love the other disciples; it was because he found his identity in the love of Jesus. "He loves... *me!*" must have been the feeling that John experienced when he was with Jesus so much so that it was how he chose to identify himself. Finding your identity in the love of another is a powerful thing that I believe is most commonly experienced by children as they relate to their parents. My little son Daniel cannot articulate much about his identity at his tender age of five years, but he could easily label himself as, "The one whom Daddy loves." And it is not just Daddy. When he is asked the question of who loves him, a sneaking smile will spread across his face as he recites, "Mama loves me, Anna loves me, Gracie loves me, Emma loves me…" and on he will go to include all the special people in his life, including grandparents, aunts, and uncles. He identifies himself by all the people who care the most about him. For the orphan this identity is lost because there are no parents to relate to. In the song "Adoption" by the band Ghost Ship, there is a point when an orphan describes the day he met his new father and he says,

> *When I met you, I didn't know you had money*
> *I didn't know you were a king*
> *I was too young to know you were a rich man*
> *I just knew you loved me*

The orphan's heart cried out for the love of a father and that desire overpowered any material want. Imagine an orphan child, after his new father visits him for the first time, being referred to by the staff or maybe by the other children as, "the one whom that father loved." Or maybe he would refer to himself, even if just in his mind, as "the one who is now loved." A new dimension has been added to his identity because of the love of a father, and that is no small thing. Despite any language or age barrier that prevents him from fully understanding the adoption process, he can understand the fact that he is loved and that his life is changed from this point forward. He is a new person with a new name and a new identity. The same is true for the lost soul who puts his or her trust in Jesus and is adopted into the family of God, becoming His beloved child. The old identity is left behind and the new identity in Christ is embraced.

I believe it is no coincidence that John, the one "whom Jesus loved," emphasized believers as "children of God" more than any other New Testament writer. Just like the orphan in the song, or my son Daniel, John experienced the love of a father for a child and rightly clung to that identity for himself personally and highlighted it in his writings. He wrote, "But to all who did receive him, who believed in his [Jesus's] name, he gave the right to become children of God" (John 1:12). In the person of Jesus, God came near to children who were not His own. In their unregenerate sinful state, they were children of another who were destined for eternal separation and isolation. God adopted them as "sons" into His home based upon the sacrifice of His Son. Christians are the children of God by vertical adoption. Because of our adoption in Christ, we can now join with John in identifying ourselves as "the ones whom God loves." No longer are we "children of wrath" but instead we are "children of promise" (Galatians 4:28) with a new Father and a new family.

LEGAL REQUIREMENTS

The adoption process is filled with legal requirements. Neither vertical adoption nor horizontal adoption is exempt from that reality. Any family who has navigated through the adoption of a child might describe these requirements as legal "red tape." Both types of adoption involve a change in the legal status of the child, and in both cases that change is significant. In the case of vertical adoption, the legal reality of our guilt before a holy and just God had to be overcome. Because of our sin, we could not have access to an absolutely righteous heavenly Father. We stood condemned, sentenced to eternal separation from the Father because of our unrighteousness. God is just, and His justice had to be satisfied in order for us to become sons through adoption. In His provision of Jesus Christ, God showed Himself to not only be just, but the Justifier of the one who has faith in Jesus (Romans 3:26). God fulfilled the need for absolute justice by providing Himself in the person of Jesus Christ to pay the price that His justice required.

For those who accept the free gift of Jesus, God imparts His righteousness to their account, clearing all debts of unrighteousness past, present, and future. "For our sake he made him to be sin who knew no sin, so that in him we might become the righteousness of God" (2 Corinthians 5:21). The legal term for this process is "justification," a word that should bring unspeakable joy to the hearts of all believers. To be justified is to be declared righteous by God and therefore free from the penalties of our sin. That in itself is an amazing statement, but it gets better. The Bible teaches the wonderful truth that justification is not the result of good works; in other words it is not earned, but it is the free gift of a loving God. "...for all have sinned and fall short of the glory of God, and are justified by his grace as a gift, through the redemption that is in Christ Jesus" (Romans 3:23–24). Justification by faith is a central tenet of Christianity, and what a glorious foundational truth it is. Because all legal requirements have been met to the fullest, we are eligible for adoption, and can enjoy a lasting fellowship in the forever family of God.

Horizontal adoption also presents us with legal realities that must be met before the adoption is finalized and the legal status of the child is changed. The legal requirements for horizontal adoption vary depending on whether the adoption is domestic or international. If the adoption is international, then further legal nuances arise depending on what country the child is being adopted from. In a Haitian adoption one of the final steps is the "adoption decree," which is a declaration that all legal requirements have been met and leads to the finalization of the process. We waited for three years before hearing the news that our adoption decree was complete. Oh, how we rejoiced on that day just like the angels in heaven rejoice at the declaration of righteousness that occurs upon the repentance of one sinner (Luke 15:10). When viewed in comparison to the legal obstacles faced by God in adopting me as his child, the paperwork we filled and the time we spent waiting seems like a small price to pay. When it comes to horizontal adoption, the words of John Piper help to put things in perspective: "If the legal red tape seems long and hard, keep in mind that this tape is not yet red with your blood—but Jesus satisfied all the legal demands precisely by shedding his blood."[1]

The law is important in both horizontal and vertical adoption. Without it, neither process could take place. If not for the fulfillment of the legal aspects of adoption, sinners would be left without access to the Father and the orphan would remain fatherless. Thank God that by His grace, He provides the solution for the legal barriers to both horizontal and vertical adoption.

THE "SONS" OF ADOPTION

"But when the fullness of time had come, God sent forth his Son, born of woman, born under the law, to redeem those who were under the law, so that we might receive adoption as sons. And because you are sons, God has sent the Spirit of his Son into our hearts, crying, 'Abba! Father!' So you are no longer a slave, but a son, and if a son, then an heir through God" (Galatians 4:4–7).

The apostle Paul used the word adoption four times in his New Testament writings (Romans 8:23, 9:4; Galatians 4:5; Ephesians 1:5). From my understanding, adoption was a relatively common practice in first-century Rome and Paul's readers would have easily understood its meaning. Though adoption was prevalent in those days, it was very different from what is has become today, and so understanding the context in which Paul used the term is important. If I was to conduct a "man on the street" interview

---

1 Dan Cruver, ed., *Reclaiming Adoption* (Adelphi, MD: Cruciform Press, 2011), 98.

tomorrow and asked for a definition of adoption, I would probably get an answer having to do with parents bringing orphan children into their homes—and that would be a correct answer in our context today. For the people in the first-century Greco-Roman world, however, the answer would be different. For them, adoption was the practice of a person with means buying out or redeeming a slave and then bringing that former slave into his own household. It was a legal transaction that freed the slave from bondage and gave him all the rights of being a son, including an inheritance. Because only male children would have any inheritance in those days, that sort of adoption was only for sons. In the context of his writing, Paul expanded the meaning of the word "sons" to include both male and female believers who now enjoyed the privilege of being children of God, having been freed from the bondage of and slavery to sin. In using the example of first-century adoption, Paul was able to highlight effectively the contrast between one who used to have a spirit of bondage but now had a spirit of "sonship," giving him or her the right to cry out "Abba! Father!"—"For you did not receive the spirit of slavery to fall back into fear, but you have received the Spirit of adoption as sons, by whom we cry, 'Abba! Father!'"(Romans 8:15). (The endearing term "Abba" is most commonly understood to be the equivalent of "Daddy." Jesus introduced this title for God during his ministry and it would have shocked the Jewish leaders because of the intimate relationship it implied.) Just as a slave would have no access to his master as a father, so the spiritually dead have no access to God the Father. But God—there is that extraordinary phrase once more— redeemed those who were hopeless and bound in chains as slaves to sin in order to adopt them as His own chil- dren. God did not just pay the redemption price and then turn us loose. It is conceivable that in Paul's day a wealthy person could have redeemed a slave and then sent him out on his own, without inviting him into his home, but that would not be adoption. Adoption, as Paul used the term, was redemption followed by sonship. God's redemp- tion was for a purpose, and that purpose was for adoption according to Galatians 4:5, where it says, "to redeem those under the law, *so that* we might receive adoption as sons" (emphasis added).

Jesus is the only Son of God by nature. All of God's other children are adopted by the redeeming work of the life, death, and resurrection of Jesus. In first-cen- tury Rome, the price for redemption was a large sum of money, but for God it was the death of His precious Son. In accepting the gift of Jesus by faith, we are united with him and become heirs in the kingdom of God. "…and if children, then heirs—heirs of God and fellow heirs with Christ, provided we suffer with him in order that we may also be glorified with him" (Romans 8:17). Because of the amazing truth of adoption, Christians have been changed from an inheritance of death to an inheritance of life.

When Paul talked about adoption, he wasn't making the case for horizontal adoption, or for parents adopting orphans, but rather he was illustrating the shift in our spiritual status as we move from slavery to sons based upon God's saving grace. He was using the common social practice of adoption in the context of his day to picture a heavenly truth. In the same way, the practice of parents adopting orphan children as understood in the current context is also useful as a picture of what God has done for believers, but with some nuanced differences compared to Paul's use of the word. The four instances where Paul used the term "adoption," while they can be helpful, are not the scriptural basis upon which horizontal adoption is modeled. It is interesting to note that even if the word "adoption" never appeared in the entire Bible, the picture of God seeking out lost children who had no hope of a future and at great cost to Himself welcoming them into His home is more than just intact; it is unmistakable. The model for horizontal adoption does not then rest on a few scattered verses in the New Testament, as important as those few verses are for salvation doctrine, but it is best found in the grand story that starts with God "In the beginning" and ends with God and His children enjoying the new heavens and a new earth together forever.

GRAFTED IN

In the book of Romans, Paul described the family of God as an olive tree (Romans 11:17–24). He used that illustration to show how the Gentiles (non-Jews) were added, or grafted in, to the family of God, which to that point only included Jews. An arborist in the first-century would have been familiar with the practice of taking a cultivated olive branch and grafting it into a wild or common tree in order to make that tree productive. The way Paul used the analogy, he flipped the common practice and "contrary to nature" talked about a wild olive branch becoming grafted into a cultivated tree. The fact that God had a plan to "graft in" outsiders, who believed in His name by faith, was the mystery that Paul revealed when he wrote, "This mystery is that the Gentiles are fellow heirs, members of the same body, and partakers of the promise in Christ Jesus through the gospel" (Ephesians 3:6).

The nation of Israel consisted of God's chosen people. They were identified primarily by their biological relationship to Abraham as his descendants: "…to them belong the adoption, the glory, the covenants, the giving of the law, the worship, and the promises. To them belong the patriarchs, and from their race, according to the flesh, is the Christ, who is God over all, blessed forever" (Romans 9:4–5). It would seem that the family tree was complete with God being the root, Abraham being the trunk so to speak, and all of his physical descendants being the branches. It would appear that the family circle was closed and all outsiders were without hope. But of course not everything is always as it appears, because Paul went on to show that it was not simply the biological descendants of Abraham who would be children of God, but only the children of the promise would enjoy that privilege. That raises the important question: Who are the children of the promise?

It was only through the line of the promised son Isaac, not any of Abraham's other children, that the promises to the nation of Israel would be fulfilled. "This means that it is not the children of the flesh who are the children of God, but the children of the promise are counted as offspring" (Romans 9:8). What was so special about the promise of Isaac? It was accepted by faith. By faith Abraham received the promise of a son who would one day become a great nation. "And he believed the Lord, and he counted it to him as righteousness" (Genesis 15:6). It was not the works of Abraham that made him righteous, but his belief in the promise of God. Therefore the true children of Abraham were not those who strictly shared a biological heritage, but only those who shared his heritage of faith. God's family is not based on physical biology but thankfully on the sharing of the *faith* of Abraham, by which even non-Jews can be grafted in to His family tree. In showing Abraham that his descendants would be as numerous as the stars in the night sky, God looked forward in time to include all those who would one day put their faith in Jesus (Genesis 15:5).

In writing to a Gentile audience, Paul reminded believers of their prior state before they were "grafted in" as children of God: "remember that you were at that time separated from Christ, alienated from the commonwealth of Israel and strangers to the covenants of promise, having no hope and without God in the world. But now in Christ Jesus you who once were far off have been brought near by the blood of Christ" (Ephesians 2:12–13). What a good thing it is for those who were far off and alienated to be brought near by the love and blood of Christ. As a Gentile living halfway around the world from the nation of Israel and thousands of years from the days of Abraham, I would be excluded as a child of God if not for this foundational truth. The family of God is composed of many different branches, both Jew and Gentile, the common denominator being their faith in Christ, not their physical heritage. That is why Galatians 3:28 can claim, "There is neither Jew nor Greek, there is neither slave nor free, there is no male and female, for you are all one in Christ Jesus."

What does any of this have to do with my family adopting two little boys from Haiti? Good question. As with the other examples we have looked at, it is all about pictures and reflections. When I consider the spiritual family tree of God, I cannot help but see a parallel developing in my own physical family tree. Our family is composed of Joelle and me as the "root," if you will, and our biological children as four natural branches. This is a seemingly closed system, because the only way to add more natural branches would be through the biological process of childbearing. God, however, just like in His own family, had a mystery to reveal. That mystery is that He can take branches that would not ordinarily be a part of my family and graft them in by means having nothing to do with biology. Those grafted branches would then have access to the same nourishing root that the natural branches enjoy without any distinction. That is adoption—taking a branch that does not "belong" and grafting it in for the purpose of belonging.

During our socialization visit to Haiti, we were interviewed in order to determine if we would be suitable adoptive parents. The interview turned into a counseling session in which a very thoughtful and well-spoken Haitian official encouraged us to show no preference for our biological kids over our adopted kids. In his mind there was to be no distinction between the natural branches and the grafted branches, and he wanted to make sure that we were all on the same page. That was obvious advice, as we would never plan to favor one child over another, but his words really struck home, not only because they were practical, but also because they were biblical.

In what has become known as "The High Priestly Prayer" found in John chapter 17, Jesus revealed a shocking truth about the love that God the Father has for his newly adopted children. In praying for those who had yet to believe but would one day respond to the Gospel message, He said, "...so that the world may know that you sent me and loved them even as you loved me" (John 17:23). "Loved them even as you loved me"? Surely that had to be some kind of mistake or at least an overstatement of the facts? How is it possible that God would lavish the same eternal, unquenchable, and overwhelming love that He has for His perfect Son on an undeserving mess like me? And yet that is exactly what Jesus said. The newly adopted children are loved with the same love the Father has for His natural Son without distinction. What an incomprehensible and wonderful thought—as the old hymn exclaims, "Amazing love! How can it be?" If God loves me in the same way that he loves Jesus, how could we not love our adopted sons with the same love that our biological children enjoy?

Despite our differences, which included not only DNA, but also culture and skin color, these boys would be a part of our family just as sure as a Gentile believer is a part of God's family. And they would be loved just the same as our biological children are loved. The grafting of children into our family may be unnatural because it does not follow normal biology, but it is also very natural as an expected reflection of the love that God shows to the outsider. By way of adoption we made those who were not "our people" our people, which is a beautiful picture of what our heavenly Father has done.

> *Those who were not my people I will call "my people," and her who was not beloved I will call "beloved."*
>
> **ROMANS 9:25**

THE PAIN OF ADOPTION

Adoption always comes at a cost. It is never free. Sacrifice is an unavoidable feature of adoption for the parent and for the child. The adopting parent must be willing to sacrifice material and emotional resources, and the adopted child must be willing to sacrifice his old life, leaving it behind as he enters into a new household. Even a small baby who is adopted must one day face the questions of why he was given up or abandoned by his parents, and that emotional cost is high. To a certain extent all adoptions are painful. Of course it is a joyous occasion when a lost child finds comfort in a new home, but there is pain involved because of the brokenness of the old home. If all was right in the world, there would be no need for any adoption because all children would be loved by present and engaged parents. Adoption is needed because the world is broken. Adoption is where the pain of brokenness and the joy of restoration meet. The adopting parent must accept and take on the pain that is present in the life of each adopted child. To adopt without entering into hurt is not to adopt. It would be like a physician treating patients but never being exposed to any illness—it is impossible. Engaging the orphan community in love is exposing oneself to the orphan's distress and inviting it into your home.

Horizontal adoption reflects a deeper and more vivid reality that is God's adoption of spiritually lost children into His family. God's adoption came at a great cost. Not only did God seek out "children of wrath" and "sons of disobedience" who were not naturally His own, but he paid for them with the sacrifice of His one and only true Son. This unfathomable sacrifice is the model for all human adoption. Just as God sacrificed in order to adopt, so must His new children sacrifice by dying to their old lives and living a new life in union with Jesus as children of God. In Christ the old has passed away and the new has come: "Therefore, if anyone is in Christ, he is a new creation. The old has passed away; behold, the new has come" (2 Corinthians 5:17). God's adoption of sinners was painful. Jesus experienced not only the excruciating (literally, because that word is derived from the pain of crucifixion) physical pain of hanging on that horrific cross but also the unbearable emotional pain of having the Father turn His face away. God was not only willing to adopt, but He was willing to enter into the pain of a broken world to rescue those He loved. The final result of God's entering into our hurt is restoration, for now of our spirits, and one day for our bodies and the rest of creation as well: "For we know that the whole creation has been groaning together in the pains of childbirth until now. And not only the creation, but we ourselves, who have the firstfruits of the Spirit, groan inwardly as we wait eagerly for adoption as sons, the redemption of our bodies" (Romans 8:22–23). If that were not enough, God's plan for His children includes sharing forever all the riches in Christ Jesus as an eternal inheritance "that is imperishable, undefiled, and unfading, kept in heaven for you" (1 Peter 1:4).

ADOPTION AND THE TRINITY

> "God's goodness is a communicative, spreading goodness…. If God had not a communicative, spreading goodness, he would never have created the world. The Father, Son and Holy Ghost were happy in themselves and enjoyed one another before the world was. But that God delights to communicate and spread his goodness, there had never been a creation nor a redemption. **God useth his creatures** not for

defect of power, that he can do nothing without them, but for the spreading of his goodness...."
—RICHARD SIBBES, 1577-1635 (EMPHASIS ADDED)

Human adoption is impossible without the Trinity. That is because both vertical adoption, God's bringing lost "sons" home, and horizontal adoption, human parents bringing orphans home, are ultimately about relationship. All relationships find their root in the Trinity, and without this root no relationships would exist. The Christian doctrine of the Trinity—that loving communion that has eternally flowed between God the Father, God the Son, and God the Holy Spirit—is the basis for all other relationships. It is the doctrine that teaches one God, but three distinct persons within that one Godhead. It is in fact the foundation of the Christian faith.

God is love—and this is only possible because of the Trinity. Love is all about relationship. "Anyone who does not love does not know God, because God is love" (1 John 4:8). Love is always moving outward, never inward (see 1 Corinthians 13). Love is never selfish, but is always directed away from the self. If there were no Trinity, God could not be love. Love cannot exist outside of a relationship, and if God is a singular personality instead of a triune personality, how would God have demonstrated His love from eternity past, before there was a creation? How does love, which always flows outward, never inward, function with no object? If God were a singular person who was not in relationship, then prior to creation, in eternity past, there would be no object of God's love and thus no love. God did not create this world to meet a need or to fill a void in Himself. God created because of the overflowing love shared among the persons of the Trinity. God, in the Trinity, existed in an eternally satisfying and exclusive family circle and yet He opened that circle, by the act of creation, to include human souls: "…In love he predestined us for adoption as sons through Jesus Christ, according to the purpose of his will" (Ephesians 1:4–5). Before the foundation of the world, God looked forward in time and—not on the basis of any merit, good deeds, or worthiness on our part—chose to include redeemed believers, by divine adoption, into His forever family. His desire was for an eternally loving relationship with His creation, even when that creation had rebelled against him in becoming "sons of disobedience" and "children of wrath" (Ephesians 2:2–3). God, in His triune relationship, by the act of creation, redemption, and adoption, is the ultimate example of outward movement, not out of need or want, but out of love.

How does human adoption model the Trinity? Our family was an exclusive circle of love held together by the bonds of biology. Of course we did not share a perfect love as exampled by God, but an imperfect human love tarnished by sin. Our family was but a dim reflection of the real thing. The six members of our home were the distinct product of Michael and Joelle Garland, making us unique, and giving us a common ground that no other family on earth shared. In some ways we could have been considered complete—two parents, four kids, one house—making us a finished family. But by the will and purpose of God, we were not compete. Through the outward movement of love, placed in us by God Himself, we were led to pursue adoption. That is, we were led to open that previously exclusive family circle we enjoyed to include two children who were on the outside. We did this because we loved them. And we loved them because God loved us. "We love because he first loved us" (1 John 4:19). We did not know our adopted children prior to beginning the process. There was nothing they had done either good or bad that influenced our pursuit of them. In a certain sense, then, like God loving us before we were yet born, we loved them before they even existed, or at least before they existed to us in a tangible way. We looked forward in time to a point in our history that their lives would intersect with ours, and in faith, by God's leading, we anticipated welcoming them into our home as adopted sons.

God is good, and in love He is spreading His goodness to the creation. In calling us to adopt, He has given to us a portion of His goodness to be used to bless the lives of the fatherless. What a wonderful God! Who can fathom His ways? To take a dull and broken instrument such as I am, and use my life to demonstrate His goodness, is a miracle that I will never fully comprehend. Here is a poem I was inspired to write while pondering my adoption into God's family and our adoption of these precious boys in light of the Trinity:

Father God,
One in Trinity.
With ever spreading goodness,
Adopted a soul like me.

In constant fellowship,
You are able to love.
The eternal relationship,
For me too high above.

With spoken Word created all,
Love spreading to all things.
And even after Adam's fall,
Mercy through the Son You bring.

Unable in my flesh,
To seek and do Your will.
With Your Spirit refresh,
My heart and soul to fill.

My heart can be so hard,
Sometimes it seems like stone.
Give me loving regard,
For those who have no home.

The source of love now overflows,
Filling up Your own.
Enabling hearts opposed to You,
To give the fatherless a home.

Not turning away Your gaze,
From little ones in need.
The orphan's lonely days,

ADOPTION: A FATHER'S STORY

Pass not Your sight unseen.

In fragile vessels like myself,
Spreading goodness is Your way.
To help me love someone else,
In my family now to stay.

MY FAMILY

MOM ALWAYS TOLD me that, "One day, a special girl will catch your eye." Well, as usual, Mom was right, because in the spring of 1995, that day happened. My sophomore year of high school was winding down quickly, as was my track and field career. Despite my best efforts I was not the track athlete I had been in junior high. It turned out that I had peaked in the eighth grade and now, two years later, the pack had not only caught up, but passed me by. Because of my lack of sprinting speed, lack of distance endurance, inability to jump high or throw far, that would be my last season of track. I did not practice well enough to earn an invitation to an official meet that year, but the season was not a total loss because of a freshman distance runner who "caught my eye."

Maybe it was her beautiful green eyes, or her playful personality, or the tenacity she showed as a freshman running alongside upperclassman at the varsity level, or a combination of things—but this young lady had my attention. Mustering all of my courage, I started my pursuit of Joelle by venturing one day into the crowded "freshman" hall at Silverton Union High School and found her at her locker. That was our first real conversation and it amounted to a "cold call" in which I asked her out on a date, having had no prior meaningful interactions with her. Clearly something was lacking in my presentation, because she promptly turned me down with the excuse that she had a "4-H meeting," which to this day seems like a creative but very unlikely story since she did not own a single animal! Well, needless to say, I persisted and eventually I was rewarded with that first date, and as they say, "The rest is history." We dated for the majority of the next three years, and I will spare you the details and drama of a teenage romance, but suffice it to say we covered the whole gamut from handwritten love letters, to long phone conversations, to breakups, and to makeups.

On August 22, 1998, we moved on from being high school sweethearts and became forever sweethearts as we said our vows and pledged our lives to one another "from that day forward, for better or for worse." Thankfully, by the grace of God, we have enjoyed much more of the "better" and very little of the "worse" over our eighteen years of marriage to date. We lived for two years as a college-aged married couple, with Joelle working and me attending classes full-time. Just about six weeks following the celebration of our second wedding anniversary, we were blessed by the birth of our daughter Anna. Over the next ten years we would experience becoming parents three more times, with the additions of Grace, Emma, and Daniel. In the pages that follow, we will be primarily focused on our two adopted children, so I want to take the opportunity here to introduce you to our biological children.

Anna Che, born October 3, 2000: Anna is a prototypical firstborn daughter who is responsible and reliable, enjoys order, and has a strong will. Being the oldest, she has been the one to break the parenting ground for us as we all learn together what it takes to raise a child. She is quick to forgive our mistakes as we try everything for the first time with her. Anna is a gifted writer and she enjoys music. At times she displays a stubborn streak, but beneath it all she has a tender heart.

Grace Madeline, born December 9, 2003: Grace is tender, compassionate, and introspective. She enjoys spontaneity in life and she is always ready for a new adventure. Her style is highlighted by an artistic flair, and she is an aspiring guitarist. At ease with babies and young children, her gentle smile and open arms have drawn many little ones into her lap for a cuddle. That gifting was particularly helpful as we visited the orphanage in Haiti and many lonely children were blessed by her presence.

Emma Joy, born November 28, 2007: As her name implies, Emma is a joy. She was born almost one year from the date that Joelle experienced a difficult miscarriage at ten weeks of pregnancy. Emma has a sweet and sensitive heart and she readily shows her emotions on her sleeve. She is quick to laugh with those who celebrate and quick to cry for those who hurt. She loves making handmade cards, playing with her little brother, and for everything in the house to be "just right." If you can catch her, Emma gives the best hugs. She thrives on routine and enjoys a song at night as she is tucked into bed and a wakeup song each morning to start the day.

Daniel Jon, born October 31, 2010: Daniel is just a fun little boy. He has grown up in a house full of women, but that has not stopped him from introducing us to Batman, Spider-Man, Transformers, and video games. He loves reading "scary" books with Mom, playing swords with anything in the house, shooting his Nerf gun, and building airplanes out of Legos. He sleeps each night in a contented coma, and he wakes each day with a smile on his face ready for a morning snuggle. Daniel has provided some masculine balance to our family and enjoys the responsibility of being the "man of the house" when I am away. He looked forward to the addition of two new adopted brothers to play with.

"Children are a gift from the Lord; they are a reward from him. Children born to a young man are like arrows in a warrior's hands. How joyful is the man whose quiver is full of them!" (Psalm 127:3–5 nlt). My children have truly been gifts from the Lord. Each of them has brought joy to Joelle and me, and after the birth of Daniel, we were well on our way to a "quiver full," having four little arrows to train up and send out. Oftentimes when a person finds out that I have four children, the response is something like, "Wow!" or "I don't know how you handle that!" or better yet, "Wait till they become teenagers!" There are occasions when that revelation sparks a more positive response, but that happens less frequently and usually comes from someone who grew up in a large family. Children can be viewed by some as a burden. While there is no doubt that having four or six children brings with it a mountain of work and responsibility, that load is outweighed by the joy those little ones bring into our lives. A snuggle in the morning, a hand-drawn picture, seeing the wonder spark in their eyes while being read to, and giving a high-five of congratulations or a hug to support a teen are examples of things I would not give up without a significant fight. Children are a joy—yes, there are hard times and lots of work is involved—but that does not diminish the beauty of a loving family. I loved my kids and I was thankful for each one of them, but in what I would characterize as a moment of little faith, I made a decision that would alter the course of our family.

As I do with many of the good gifts God provides in this life, I began to think of them in terms of my own will instead of in terms of God's will. I began to place my own purpose and plan for my family above God's purpose and plan for us. Joelle and I had been used to "raised eyebrows" over getting married right out of high school. But now we were facing a second round of perceived criticism for having so many children. In a culture where two children is the norm, having four definitely stands out. That "eyebrow raising" in combination with Joelle's sore back after her fourth full-term pregnancy led me to take a stumble of faith and schedule that appointment that makes all men cringe—a vasectomy. The reason I characterize that decision as a "stumble" is because it was an effort to place my priorities above God's when it came to having more children.

I am not one who would say that God is against all forms of birth control. But there was something different about the vasectomy. Perhaps it was the fact that it involved an uncomfortable surgical procedure that I wanted to avoid, but I believe it was more than that. I remember very clearly leaving our house and driving to the clinic on the "big day" and just not feeling right about it. My conscience, or perhaps more accurately the Holy Spirit, was telling me to turn around. All believers have had the feeling at one time or another that they are doing something wrong, and yet with perseverance of will, they push past the Spirit's objections and continue on their chosen path. Well, that day seemed to be my day to exert my own will despite my conscientious objections. It is easy to rationalize and just chalk up the doubts to nervousness, and that is what I did as I walked into the clinic that day. I checked in, completed the procedure, and walked out having accomplished my purpose, which was to limit the number of children in our family. The problem was not so much what I had done. I am not making the argument that birth control is always wrong. It was my action despite God's leading otherwise that troubled me. I had no idea that God was planning to use, what I now describe as a poor decision, for a greater good. Adoption was nowhere on my radar screen during that time. I wish I could say that our plans all along included bringing more children into our home, but that was simply not true. I thought our family was complete with four kids, but God knew we had room for two more.

God, in his amazing sovereignty, can take our mistakes and use them for his glory. He is big enough to put together the broken pieces of our failures and build something beautiful from them. As we saw earlier, God used the shortcomings of the nation of Israel to accomplish the mystery of His will that was to include (non-Jewish) Gentiles as His children. As they say, "God works in mysterious ways." I do not fully understand how all of the events in my life fit together to fulfill God's purpose in me, but my decision to artificially (and somewhat permanently) halt God's blessed gift of children opened the door for us to consider adoption. I don't know what would have happened if I had not followed through with the procedure, but I believe that if we had even one more biological child, we would have been much less likely to pursue adoption. To this day I am not comfortable with my decision because I believe it was displeasing to God. I am humbled and thankful, however, that God in His grace used my shortcomings to bring two sweet boys into our lives.

We would not begin thinking seriously about adoption until two years later. With the tender love of a mother's heart, even though she was busy with our four children at home, Joelle began to hurt for the fatherless (and motherless). On several occasions she brought up the subject of adoption, which I commended as a noble pursuit for other people, but not for us. It was too expensive, there were too many unknowns, it would hurt our biological children, we were not ready, we didn't have the space, and other such objecting thoughts filled my mind whenever the subject came up. Compared to her, I saw myself as the one who was thinking practically with his "feet on the ground," so to speak. Adopting orphan children was a wonderful thing, but I just did not see how it would work for our family; the barriers seemed too tall and too many. Joelle respected my hesitations and concerns, many of which she also shared, so we just waited and prayed. Truth be told, I figured the whole "adoption phase" would pass as we focused in on our already busy lives.

I cannot really explain what happened next other than to say that I know it happened. Have you ever tried to remember the exact moment in which you fell asleep? There is no doubt that it occurred, because you woke some hours later, hopefully refreshed by a peaceful slumber. But the transition from being awake to being asleep is always sort of vague, isn't it? If anything could be vague, but also undeniably certain, it may be the moment of sleep. It just sort of happens and you don't realize it until after the fact. In the same way, the transition in my heart from being reluctant to adopt to embracing the idea in full was certain, but I cannot say exactly how or when it happened.

The only explanation I can give is that we prayed and waited, and God answered in a way that I never expected. We experienced no drama of any handwriting on the wall or a voice speaking from heaven. It was a simple change of heart that He caused. More than that, it was a small piece of His heart that He gave me as I began to see the fatherless as He does. Those children mattered to God, and as His hands and feet in this world, He had given me the opportunity to care for them. The more I thought about those who are without hope or home, the more I saw myself and the state I was in spiritually before God invited me into His family. In one sense I was an orphan, but God rescued me. That realization changed my attitude from "How can I adopt?" to "How can I not adopt?" God had stirred up a love within me that had not been there before, and that new love was about to change our family forever.

When I think back on our decision to adopt, I see that it was more God's doing than my own. Therefore, if there is any glory to be had in this adoption story, it all belongs to God, because He is the Author. And He wrote not just my story but the *whole* story of history in which His love is the central theme. That is why I am writing this book; not so much to tell my story, but God's. My story as *a father* is only worthwhile in so far as it points you to the story of *the Father*. It could be that you are a spiritual orphan in need of a father, and I would seek to point you to the one who would sacrifice His very life to first redeem you, and then adopt you into His family.

WHY HAITI?

IN THE SPRING of 2013 our official adoption journey began. We set out on that adventure having no idea how we would reach our destination. In fact we did not even know where exactly the destination was, but we traveled in peace knowing that God was in control.

As people around us heard about what we were doing, one of the most common questions we were asked was, "Why Haiti?" Early on in the process I was always at a loss for how to answer. I would stumble through some rambling incoherent reasons as I watched just the slightest look of bewilderment creep into their expression as if they wanted to say, "You really don't know why you chose to adopt from Haiti? Maybe you should give this some more thought." Of course no one ever actually said that, but I always had the feeling that I left people wanting when they asked that very simple question of "Why Haiti?"

Now that I have had more time to reflect on our decision to pursue a Haitian adoption, the answer is very clear
to me even though it may seem inadequate to some. We
were not motivated by the devastating earthquake of 2010
that shook an already struggling nation to its knees. It was
not a mission trip during which we fell in love with the
Haitian people that made us want to adopt. We had no
connection to a friend or family member who had adopted
from Haiti. There was no pre-identified child who stole our
hearts. We were not directed by an adoption agency to the
region of the world where the need for adoptive parents
was the greatest. No one in our church family encouraged
us to consider Haiti. Even our own parents, who would be
the grandparents of our adopted kids, did not steer us to
any country in particular. None of these things drew us to
Haiti. The reason we chose Haiti—the one driving force
behind our decision—was Wikelson and Richardson. It's
really that simple: we chose to adopt from Haiti because of
our love for Wikelson and Richardson.

Wikelson (Wee – kale – son) and Richardson (Ree –
shard – son) were ages three and one respectively when
they entered the BRESMA orphanage in January 2014.
They came from a suburb of Port-au-Prince called Cite
Soleil, one of the most impoverished and dangerous com-
munities in all of Haiti, where there are no sewers and
many of the homes are constructed of nothing but sal-
vaged garbage material. Upon their arrival both boys were
underweight, malnourished, and anemic. Richardson had
an active hepatitis A infection that is most commonly

contracted from drinking water contaminated by human feces. He was also suffering from giardia (an intestinal parasite) and a bacterial external ear infection. (We would later find out that Wikelson also had a chronic giardia infection as well as latent tuberculosis that required 9 months of antibiotics to cure.) Having no family able to care for them, they were placed with the nannies at the orphanage with the hope that one day they would find a stable and safe home to grow up in. They had many material needs, like food, clean water, and shelter, but they also needed love, and in His infinite wisdom God placed the very love that they needed into the hearts of Joelle and me as He led us to pursue adoption.

There is only one problem with this otherwise very reasonable answer to the question of "Why Haiti?" The problem is that we did not know who Wikelson and Richardson were until about two and a half years into the adoption process. We started in the spring of 2013 and we did not meet them until November of 2015. Haitian adoptions rarely involve pre-identified children. Instead you commit to adopting and then find out later along the way whom you will be bringing into your home. In that way it is very much like a normal pregnancy. Nobody chooses their children and then becomes pregnant. Biologic parents never find out who their children are until after they have committed to having them sight unseen. So the question of "Why Haiti" or "Why Wikelson and Richardson?" is sort of like asking "Why Anna, Grace, Emma, or Daniel?" If someone had asked Joelle back in 2000, "Why are you going through this pregnancy?" the answer would have been, "Because we love Anna," even though we had not yet met her (or named her). The reason we have each of our children is because God chose to bless us with them.

Claiming that we were motivated by boys we had never met seemed like an irreconcilable contradiction that created more problems than it solved. While that may have been a problem for human thinking, it was no problem at all for God. Some might say that it was impossible for us to base our adoption decision on children we did not know, and they would be right: "With man it is impossible, but not with God. For all things are possible with God" (Mark 10:27). God was in control and He knew exactly the two brothers He had planned to be a part of our family, just as He knew exactly the four biological children He would give us.

As we prayed for direction during the decision-making process, I never heard an audible voice, had a dream, or experienced some other dramatic sign, but God accomplished His will through our availability. Citing God's providence as the answer to why we chose Haiti may seem mystical or like an exaggerated religious cliché, but I believe it is true without a doubt. Frankly I was uncertain myself of why we chose Haiti until I met the boys, and then, with tears in my eyes, I dropped to my knees in thanksgiving to God for His faithful leading. Our faith was small, but His provision was abundant, and those boys stole our hearts on the very first day we met.

Here is a poem I wrote as I waited for God to reveal His purpose for us in Haiti:

My heart beats in a distant land,
Connected to another far away.
Reaching in love for a little hand,
The heart of the Father on display.

My soul pierced by the orphan's need,
Though I know not name or face.
Privileged to love, clothe, and feed,
And to provide a safe place.

My spirit hurts for children that lost,
No parents to guide and care.
When considering my own little cost,
It does not even compare.

Not by my strength but on my knees,
Seeking my peace in You.
While caring for the least of these,
Finding religion pure and true.

Religion that is pure and undefiled before God the Father is this: to visit orphans and widows in their affliction, and to keep oneself unstained from the world.

JAMES 1:27

GREATER THAN THE UNIVERSE?

IN REFERENCE TO God's knowledge that He would redeem and adopt lost souls before the creation, John Piper once said that "Adoption is greater than the universe."[2] When we first started our adoption journey, I may have differed with Dr. Piper on that particular point. I think what he meant to say was that the *paperwork required* to complete an adoption was greater than the universe. There are so many hoops to jump through, appointments to make, fees to pay, "I's" to dot and "T's" to cross, that it is a wonder anyone ever finishes it all. Our process took so long that we had to do three home studies because they kept expiring! But just like completing a long and difficult hike, we just kept putting one foot in front of the other and over time we saw forward progress as our "to do" list became shorter and shorter.

2 Dan Cruver, "Adoption Is Bigger Than You Think," accessed October 10, 2016, http://www.desiringgod.org/articles/adoption-is-bigger-than-you-think.

As we moved slowly closer to the completion of the adoption, the gravity of what we were doing became very real to me. This was more than just the addition to our family of two children from a different culture, as complicated as that might have been. What once felt like something *I* was doing soon became much bigger than me. I was discovering that I was not breaking new ground, but rather following a path that had been prepared for me from long ago—maybe even from before the creation itself!

We live in Oregon, which is famous for the Oregon Trail that pioneers followed as they made their trek westward. There are still some places along the trail that even today you can see the wheel ruts where wagon after wagon traveled the path that had been taken by those who had gone before. How reassuring it must have been for the settlers, who left their homes and all that was familiar to them, to see that trail ahead providing evidence that the journey could indeed be completed. As we ventured along the path of adoption, I was not blazing a new trail as if I was leading my family on some noble humanitarian mission. On the contrary, with each step my foot fell into footprints that had been laid down long ago so that I could walk in them. Someone had gone before me. The path I was following was not my own but God's, because He had prepared the way. The more I realized that, the more I was filled with the same confidence that those who traveled the Oregon Trail must have had when they saw the ruts ahead of them. It is important to point out that just because others had first traveled that trail, it did not mean the going would be easy, and it certainly wasn't for many of those brave pioneers. They likely experienced many instances when, staring in disbelief at a steep canyon or rushing river, they looked fearfully at the trail ahead in awe that anyone had successfully passed before them. In the same way, just because God was leading me, it did not guarantee ease in the journey, because His paths are usually filled with difficulty. Just take a look at the heroes of the faith in ancient or modern times and try to find one who was not called into hardship. While my faith was far from heroic, it was my privilege to walk in the works that God had prepared, even if the road would be bumpy at times: "For we are his workmanship, created in Christ Jesus for good works, which God prepared beforehand, that we should walk in them" (Ephesians 2:10).

In that regard our adoption was "greater than the universe" because God had laid its foundation from before time began. And by the way, it is not just me, or our adoption, but everything in my life and yours that God is using for His ultimate glory. In reading my account, you may have the impression that I see myself on a special mission sent by God. That is true; however, it is not just me, but all Christians are called to the good works that God has for us and all non-Christians are invited to enter into the grace of God through the acceptance of Jesus His Son. This story is about my participation in the work that God has done, and my intention is that He gets any and all glory that results from it.

COUNTING THE COST

The Lord will provide.
GENESIS 22:14

ADOPTION IS VERY expensive. Prior to starting this process, we knew there would be significant financial obligations and we thought we were ready to meet that challenge. What we did not anticipate was the emotional cost of loving faraway fatherless children who were separated from us by geographical distance and procedural bureaucracy. We believed that God had chosen two specific children to join our family, and it brought us pain and frustration to imagine them spending day after day without a father or mother. Before we knew their names or saw their faces, we hurt for them as if they were our own. One lesson we learned is that God will provide. Ultimately, like all things, our adoption story was in His hands and He provided for us in ways that we could never have imagined. In the end our financial and emotional reserves were not deep enough (not even close) but God's were. This was His story after all, and through each step along the way, He gently taught us to trust in Him. I sincerely believe that if we had known before we started the extent of the financial and emotional burden this process would involve, we would not have signed up. Of course we "knew" the cost would be high; we just didn't understand exactly how high. It was like the difference between watching somebody else jump off a bridge into a lake and then actually doing it yourself. The bridge is much higher when it is your own toes extending out from the edge and you look down to the water below. When it came to the financial challenges we faced, God allowed us to fall into some very precarious places so that His provision would be unmistakable. While we did sacrifice during the process, it is my feeling that God did not want us to do this alone. He wanted the work of His hand to be evident.

As I think back on our journey, I'm reminded of the faithful provision that God showed to Abraham as he climbed Mount Moriah with his son Isaac (Genesis 22). Abraham was an old man. He had waited most of his life for a son, a promised one who would make of him a great nation. It must have been incredibly perplexing when God commanded him to sacrifice his son Isaac, destroying his hope for future generations. But Abraham had faith. He trusted that God would provide, and even when Abraham did not see any possible way of sparing his son, he obeyed

God. Of course God did provide a ram, his horns caught in a thicket, sparing Isaac, who would go on to become a patriarch for the nation of Israel. Centuries later God the Father would climb that same mountain with His only Son, Jesus, except this time the Son would not be spared (Romans 8:32) but would become the sacrificial lamb and by His death on the cross provide a way to salvation by the power of the resurrection to all who would believe: "For God so loved the world, that he gave his only son, that whoever believes in him should not perish but have eternal life" (John 3:16). Both in supplying the ram for Abraham and Jesus His beloved Son for all humanity, God showed His abundant provision. Abraham named that mountain, "The Lord will provide," and indeed He did.

Oh that I had the faith of Abraham! I believed that God wanted us to travel the road of adoption, and yet there was still a whisper of doubt lingering in my mind. I could easily echo the father in Mark 9:24, who said, "I believe; help my unbelief!" But despite my lack of complete faith, God was and is faithful. Jesus said that faith the size of a mustard seed could move mountains (Mathew 17:20). While I do not know what seed is smaller than the mustard seed, I know my faith was not the mountain-moving sort. But God took my meager belief—my weak and sometimes dysfunctional faith—and provided for us richly for His glory and for my spiritual growth. When it came to the financial expenses for international adoption, I thought I could provide for myself. I thought that by careful planning and saving, we would not need God's intervention in the provision of monetary resources. After all, I thought, God had provided me with a good job, and if I just worked hard and spent wisely, we could do this on our own.

God took this mind-set I had and used it for my growth and for His glory. The costs were more than I had expected, other more immediate financial obligations came up, and at times I was not as disciplined as I thought I would be at saving. Despite our best efforts we were falling behind, and I'm so thankful that we did. God used my shortcomings as an opportunity to place a gentle hand on my shoulder, encourage me to my knees in prayer, and teach me reliance upon Him. It turns out that, spiritually speaking, it is very healthy when we say, "I cannot do this on my own." God was asking me to demonstrate a greater faith so that He could show His glory through greater provision. There are few things more encouraging and strengthening to a Christian's faith than to rely completely on God and then see Him answer in amazing ways. And when it comes to glory, I can take none for myself if I know that I did not accomplish anything, but it was God working in my life that accomplished everything. Because of our financial struggles, I grew in my faith and God was more glorified in the process! What an amazing heavenly Father!

Two distinct instances of divine provision stood out among the rest. The remarkable thing is that there were probably dozens of ways that God provided for us here and there, but we just failed to recognize them because they occurred behind the scenes. At any rate, two dramatic examples were beyond a doubt the work of God. In His divine omniscience, God planned the intersecting of two lives into our adoption story in a way that only He could do. I had never before received an inheritance from the passing of a family member and I had no reason to believe that any such event was imminent. And yet on two separate occasions, at just the right time, God provided almost embarrassing amounts of inheritance money to practically fall from the sky and into our adoption account. Two loved ones finished their courses, both running races that brought honor to God, and God used their entrance into glory to, among other things, provide some of the needed funds for our adoption. Our God is so incredible. It's not that He caused death in order to provide for us; it's that He had each detail of those two faithful lives planned, woven throughout His great story, each event meaningful and ordained by Him. Each of them touched hundreds, perhaps thousands of people during their lifetimes as they lived out God's Word. The fact that God orchestrated their passings to intersect with the moment of our need is nothing short of a miracle.

I will share a few details about one of these episodes. Let's fast-forward for a moment to the time shortly after our first trip to Haiti to meet our boys. We had arrived home anticipating a long wait before we could return to finally claim them as our own. Our adoption savings were about 75 percent drained from the travel costs and international adoption fees due during our visit. Because the following steps were normally very drawn out, we expected to have time to replenish our savings before the next big installment was due. Well, we had been praying that God would move things along quickly without major delays, and once again He answered. The biggest hurdle was the approval of our socialization visit by the Haitian adoption authorities, and that step was supposed to take about four months. After six weeks we got an email from our agency telling us we had been approved—way ahead of schedule. With that approval came due a large (and final) international fee. It was money that we did not have. We had some reserve in our savings but not enough to cover what was required. We were thankful that the process was moving, but we did not see a way to pay that bill without borrowing from someone, using credit, or dipping into 401(k) savings.

It was a Tuesday. I gathered the family together in our living room to discuss the situation and have a time of prayer. We prayed to God, admitting that we did not have the resources on our own, and relied on His provision. I knew that He wanted this adoption to happen, but frankly I did not see one source of extra money anywhere in our future other than going into debt. Our prayer ended and we went our separate ways, waiting to see what God would do. As we waited, once again I felt like Abraham, but this time in a negative way. When God promised Abraham a son, he believed God, but not completely. After waiting years without the arrival of a son, Abraham took matters into his own hands, attempting to fulfill the promise by having a son with Sarah's maidservant Hagar. Abraham believed, but he did not wait for God's timing. In my case I began to seek out answers to our financial pinch on my own, rather than waiting to see what God would do (or in this case what God had already done). I approached the financial manager at my office to find out if I could withdraw funds from my 401(k) and use them for the adoption. The answer was "No" because safeguards had been put in place to keep employees from drawing down their accounts prior to retirement (probably a good idea). Then I turned to my dad. Perhaps he and Mom would be willing to front me some money and I could pay them back later? At the time I did not feel at peace about these efforts, but I told myself this was a desperate situation and I had to do something. Like Abraham, this was my Hagar moment. Abraham also was desperate and he thought he would help God by moving things along on his own.

It turned out that God already had a plan to provide for us before the need ever arose. If I had just waited! If Abraham had just waited! God would have provided without my (and Abraham's) pitiful efforts. We prayed for provision on a Tuesday, and by Saturday of the same week, we were informed that a large check was in the mail, a check that was coming to us before we ever asked, and a check that would more than cover the fees due. We were receiving an inheritance and it was not just monetary. That check provided not only for our material need at the time but it also represented a heritage of faith that was being passed down to us by one of God's good and faithful servants. My grandma had entered into God's glory, but the life she had lived continued to be a blessing to my family and the two new additions we were anticipating. "Now to him who is able to do far more abundantly than all we ask or think...to him be glory..." (Ephesians 3:20). With a humbled heart I gave thanks to God, understanding more each day that the journey was much bigger than me.

OPPOSITION

I NEVER FULLY REALIZED the stranglehold my flesh had on my spirit until the adoption. Paul described the flesh as the part of his being in which nothing good dwelled: "For I know that nothing good dwells in me, that is, in my flesh. For I have the desire to do what is right, but not the ability to carry it out" (Romans 7:18). For the Christian the flesh has been described as an unwelcome roommate who is persistently present and doing everything possible to distract us from fulfilling the will of God in our lives. The victory that is mine in Christ Jesus frees me from the power of the flesh, but (for now) not from its presence. It is the part of me that must be denied daily in order to let the new creation that is my life in Christ shine forth: "Therefore, if anyone is in Christ, he is a new creation. The old has passed away; behold, the new has come" (2 Corinthians 5:17; see also Romans 6:5–6; Galatians 2:20). It is a battle that I thought I had been successfully fighting, but in taking the step of faith to adopt, I encountered an overwhelming fleshly assault on my spirit that I did not see coming.

Within myself a war is raging between the new man and the old, between the spirit and the flesh, and never was this more obvious than in the days following "the call." Our adoption story was an incredibly long journey, spanning more than three years from start to finish. During the first two years our adoption reality consisted of paperwork, more paperwork, financial obligations, more paperwork, home studies, and dreaming of who our new children would be. We had no pictures, names, or descriptions to focus on. We did not even know for sure the gender of the kids, although we had requested that one be a boy. In those days our concept of adopting was completely abstract with nothing to ground it in the reality of our actual lives. It was a dream and a desire. It was a commitment we had made, a journey we had started, but we really knew nothing of the destination we were headed for. It was a leap of faith. Of course, we knew it was serious and we had tried to do our due diligence in learning as much as we could about bringing new children into our home. But it wasn't until "the call" that reality (and the battle) began to strike home.

From the day our application was accepted into the Haitian government social services in the spring of 2014, we had waited for "the call." As we waited, the Lord was working behind the scenes through our adoption agency to set up a potential match between our family and two orphan children. Our agency director had informed us that the process would be lengthy, but that once the government had approved the proposed match, she would call us and give us all the information about our new kids. It was a day that we looked forward to both with a sense of anticipation of joy and with the uneasiness of doubt. We wanted so badly to discover who God had planned to join our family, but what if we didn't love them? What if there were behavioral or health problems that we hadn't planned on? What if we didn't see them as cute (awful to ask but an honest concern)? What if they rejected us as parents? On the other hand, what if we loved them too much? What if our efforts to bring them into our home would damage the relationships we had with our biological children? With these questions left to simmer, we waited…and waited…and waited.

Do you remember *The Lion, The Witch and the Wardrobe* by C. S. Lewis? In the land of Narnia, before the return of Aslan, it was always winter, but never Christmas. Imagine a child waiting patiently all winter for a Christmas that never arrived. That is how we felt about "the call." We waited and waited and waited and it did not come. We heard about other Haitian adoptions moving forward but our "call" never came. We waited so long that we nearly stopped anticipating. Slowly friends and family stopped asking if we had heard any news and we almost stopped believing that we ever would. I became very pragmatic at that point, considering the possibility that we were headed down the wrong path and that the long delay was God's way of stopping us before we made a huge mistake. Perhaps we had mistaken our calling to adopt and God was shutting the door? Of course we know that God's timing rarely matches our expectation and that He has plans for us that are often bigger than our meager imaginations. The "call" finally did come, and it is a day I will not soon forget.

A birthday party is a joyous, busy, and sometimes crazy event in the life of a family—especially if that birthday party is for a five-year-old little boy. Special events like these remind me how proud and privileged I am to be a father. They also remind me of the love I have for my kids. It is hard for me to fully describe that love. To be sure, it is more than just a feeling. It is an intertwining of my soul with theirs in the bond of fatherly love. When they hurt, I hurt. When they are sick, I am sick. And just the smallest thought of one of them suffering or dying causes my spirit to melt. If my love is deep for my children, how much more is the Father's love unfathomably deep for the Son. I cannot imagine sacrificing my child to save the life of another, and yet that is what Father God did when He sent His Son, Jesus, to die in my place on that horrific cross. How much also must God love me, his child by adoption, whom He sought out and rescued when I was lost?

Now, returning to the birthday party. Daniel was turning five and we anticipated a day of superhero capes, games of chase, fun treats, and opening presents with friends and relatives. The party was to start in the early afternoon, and I had run out to complete some errands in the midmorning. As I arrived home, I looked at my phone and noticed that I had missed five calls—all from Joelle. *Oh great,* I thought. *What did I forget at the store?* My eyes then focused on

Emma, who was seven at the time, sheepishly walking outside along the wall of our front porch.

I stepped away from the car and said, "Hey, Emma," as I casually walked to the front door.

"We got the call" she said in a soft and sweet seven-year-old princess voice.

"What? The call…What call?" I replied, having no idea what she was talking about. I gathered my things and headed toward the door.

"We got the call," she repeated, a little more assertive this time.

"Who called?" My brain searched for the missing piece as I tried to put this puzzle together.

"We got the call for the boys, and it's them. It's Wikelson and Richardson."

Then it hit me. As I write this story months after the fact, it still hits me, bringing tears to my eyes. *The* call. *The* boys. The absolute faithfulness of God in showing us tender mercy during our seemingly endless wait. You see, those were not just any boys—some random fatherless kids whose names I learned that day. Those were the boys that we had been following, and watching, and loving from afar as we dreamed they might be our match. Over the previous months we had enjoyed looking through pictures other parents would post as they traveled to the same orphanage in Haiti that our children called home. Because we knew there was a match for us and that they lived at that orphanage, it was fun to look at the pictures of the kids and try to figure out which ones might be ours. Over time we grew attached to two sweet boys who we assumed must be brothers. We knew this was dangerous, and despite the chance of disappointment, we sort of began considering those boys our own. Any time new pictures came through, we would search for them, think about them, pray for them, and love them. We did try to steel our hearts against a letdown, and provide room for the possibility that God had other children in mind for us. If that was the case, we wanted to be fair to them, not wishing they were somebody else when the call came. Despite these efforts Wikelson and Richardson enjoyed a special place in our home as we waited to finally meet our "official" kids. We grew so fond of them that we tried to skirt the rules of Haitian adoption by writing an email of inquiry to our program director trying to find out more about them. We figured that if we found out their relationship to one another and their ages, it might give us a better idea if they fell within the parameters we had been approved for. After a firm scolding from our agency denying our request (we found out later that our director was surprised we had guessed who our match was and she wanted to share that news with us but couldn't), we gave up on playing detective and continued to pray that God would send us exactly the right children for our family.

We knew them before they knew us. We loved them and cared for them when they had no concept that a father and mother were on the way. There they were, living their broken, incomplete lives, having no idea that love was coming from afar to bring them home. For the Christian, that parallels the truth taught in Scripture that God "chose us in him before the foundation of the world.... In love he predestined us for adoption to himself as sons through Jesus Christ..." (Ephesians 1:4–5). The mystery of that truth is great, as is the overwhelming love the Father shows for His children, choosing them before they did anything good or bad, and choosing them before the creation itself. We did not see God coming, but He loved us from afar, and broke into our world in the person of Jesus Christ to rescue us and provide for us a forever home with the Father above. Praise God for His profound love for us!

On October 31, 2015, Daniel Garland's fifth birthday, we got "the call" that would change our lives, and the lives of two little boys forever. Joelle took the call, and sitting down, head in hands, she was speechless but softly crying as she listened to the news of two boys—Wikelson, age five, and Richardson, age three—who were homeless and helpless, who needed a forever family, and who had been chosen specifically for us. We didn't want this special news to take center stage and rob Daniel of any of his five-year-old birthday joy, but then what better gift could a little boy, who lived in a house full of girls, get than two brothers to play rough-and-tumble with? So we celebrated Daniel that day and we celebrated the awesome news that he would soon have two brothers that would equalize the balance of power in our home—six kids, with three girls and three boys.

That is when my flesh, that ever-present enemy, joined by the spiritual forces of darkness—neither of which wanted that adoption to happen—organized for a full frontal assault on my spirit, mind, and body. Paul wrote in the letter to the Ephesians that a spiritual war is waged against believers: "For we do not wrestle against flesh and blood, but against the rulers, against the authorities, against the cosmic powers over this present darkness, against the spiritual forces of evil in the heavenly places" (Ephesians 6:12). It seems reasonable to believe that these forces will attack most aggressively when a believer is taking a step of faith. If you are waging a war, you concentrate your forces where the enemy is most active, and that is exactly what Satan does. As I stepped out of the barracks of belief and onto the battlefield of action, the raging war became all the more real to me. I grew up listening to the song "Beyond Belief" by the Christian rock band Petra, and twenty-five years after first hearing it, the meaning finally hit home. At that time, more than any other, I was going beyond belief allowing God to do His "boots on the ground" work through me. In taking the step of faith to adopt these precious boys, I was breaking ranks with my flesh and placing my life in the line of enemy fire. I did not fully understand the implications of that decision until we got "the call" and the adoption process changed in character from a distant desire to an impending reality. We had names. We knew faces. These kids were real and they were in desperate need. God had called me, as the head of our family, to stand in the gap, providing for and protecting them by welcoming them into our home. More than that, God had called me to raise them in the "discipline and instruction of the Lord" (Ephesians 6:4), and that is something Satan would surely try to thwart.

Haitian adoption law required a two-week socialization

visit prior to finalization of a proposed parent-child match. The purpose was to give us an opportunity to interact with the children under the supervision of the adoption authorities. Now that we knew the boys we had been matched with, we were cleared to schedule that important visit. Following that step, we were told to expect up to a twelve-month wait before we could return and finally bring them home as Garland kids. My personal spiritual battle began as we planned that socialization trip to Haiti. It started with fear. Crushing, paralyzing fear would torment me over the three weeks leading up to our travel date. My anxieties found their root in things as simple as travel sickness and leaving Daniel and Emma for two weeks, as well as in complicated concerns of ruining my family, finances, and future. A constant barrage of feelings of inadequacy for the task at hand had me shaken deeply. I was so excited and thankful to learn of the boys that God had chosen for us, and yet I was carrying a heavy burden. My flesh had become a dead weight that was anchored firmly to the ground and refused to be moved except by tremendous effort.

I never realized the love I had for my comfortable life until taking just the first step away from it. In some respects my family seemed to be complete. I had a good job. We had a good marriage. Joelle enjoyed the routine and rhythm of homeschooling our kids, who all seemed healthy and happy. We were an active part of our church and were blessed to have loving and close relationships with extended family both far and near. By some standards we had it made. *Why risk all this?* my troubled heart would ask. *You have so much to lose. It's not worth it.* Separating the desires of my flesh from the desires of my spirit at first seemed an insurmountable task. I felt as though my flesh was so inseparably bonded to my spirit that it could not be removed without severely damaging both. I was beginning to understand more deeply why Paul wrote, "For I do not do the good I want, but the evil I do not want is what I keep on doing" (Romans 7:19). This epic wrestling match that even the writer of most of the New Testament struggled with had become mine on a new and more profound level. It's not that I had never grappled with my flesh or faced spiritual opposition before; it's just that I had never faced such a motivated flesh or such a formidable spiritual foe. *You are not strong enough. You don't have enough faith for this. You don't have enough love for them,* the voice of my flesh kept whispering in my ear.

I will admit that this voice had a grain of truth in it. It was a twisted half-truth used to knock me off my course, but it was truth nonetheless. It wasn't until I realized that the enemy was right, at least in some sense, that I began to find a deep comfort. I was not strong enough, nor did I have enough faith, nor did I have enough love in my heart to bring these boys into my home. About these things my flesh had rightly accused me. But God was strong, and He would give me faith when I lacked it, and He had more than enough overflowing love to pour out for these little ones. No, it was not by my strength that the mission would be accomplished, but only by the strength He would supply. The task was more than I could handle—that was a fact—but I was not alone.

It was through that process of separation and growing I

learned that, on my own, I did not have the strength to lead my family, love my four biological kids, or love my wife the way Christ loved the church, being willing to die to myself to see her built up. It was not just in the adoption process that I was helpless on my own, but my entire life needed to be surrendered to God. Oftentimes my mind-set was that I would control the routine aspects of my life and then ask God to help with the heavy lifting when needed. The adoption was helping me to see the fallacy in that way of thinking. I was being exposed for what I really am—utterly lost without God. The old hymn, "I Need Thee Every Hour," played often in my mind in those days, reminding me that I was weak but God was strong. With that weakness came not shame but a contented confidence. Of course a measure of pride had to be put down as I faced my shortcomings, but what I found was far superior to any strength I could claim as my own: "For the sake of Christ, then, I am content with weaknesses…. For when I am weak, then I am strong" (2 Corinthians 12:10). Admitting my weakness was the allowance of God's strength to work in me and there was no firmer foundation on which to stand than that.

In my struggle to stop clinging to my life, I was reminded that Jesus, though He was equal with God, did not cling to or hold fast to that position, but readily gave it up, becoming as a servant to complete His mission. In comparison I was giving up so little to complete my mission, and in reality what I sacrificed (my selfish life) was damaging to me and had no potential to provide me with lasting happiness in the end. "Have this mind among yourselves, which is yours in Christ Jesus, who, though he was in the form of God, did not count equality with God a thing to be grasped, but emptied himself, by taking the form of a servant, being born in the likeness of men. And being found in human form, he humbled himself by becoming obedient to death, even death on a cross" (Philippians 2:5–8). Jesus humbled Himself, leaving an exalted position in the heavenly kingdom to take on the frailty of human flesh. In coming to walk on the earth, He did not hold fast to the standing that He had but let it go in order to complete His mission. If that is my God, how can I not give up my rule over the pretend kingdom that is my life in order to complete the work that He has called me to?

The opposition I faced was not just emotional or spiritual; it was also physical. I had never experienced hip pain before. Because I worked as an orthopedic physician assistant in a specialty hip and knee practice, my days were spent caring for patients with sore joints. Over the years I had heard countless stories of that deep aching pain in the front of the hip joint that so disrupts a person's life. Therefore I found it quite ironic that about ten days before leaving for Haiti, my right hip began to hurt in the absence of any injury, overuse, or other event that could account for it. I grew up playing sports and I was used to the occasional sore shoulder or knee. As I began to push forty years of age, even my low back would gripe at me from time to time. That hip pain was different. It was a new problem that I had not yet had to deal with.

The pain was so severe that I was not able to sleep at night. As if I did not have enough nervous thoughts robbing me of sleep, now I had a dull aching hip to further disrupt my rest. What's more, exercise is one of my primary coping techniques to deal with stress, and because of my hip I was not able to have that outlet in the days leading up to the most stressful "vacation" of my life. I don't know if that pain was a thorn in the flesh or a "messenger of Satan" (2 Corinthians 12:7). All I know is that it was the piling on of physical stress to the already considerable load of emotional stress I was carrying. It bothered me throughout the visit to Haiti, making me think twice about climbing stairs at the orphanage or kicking a ball with the boys, as well as keeping me up at night. (Make of it what you will, but my hip pain did not begin to resolve until about 10 months later when the boys at last arrived home.) Before we began our adoption journey, we heard from other adoptive parents that there would be opposition to the process. I largely blew that off as over-spiritualization of coincidental events that would have taken place whether or not those people had been adopting. As I reflect back on my own experience, however, I can no longer blame coincidence for the opposition that I found in front of me. Adoption is an uphill battle that is met with stiff resistance from the enemy of everything that is good.

I am convinced that Satan hates adoption. He stands

against all that would image the glory of God and His love, and human adoption falls into that category. Not only was he opposed to our adoption of Wikelson and Richardson, he is violently opposed to God the Father's adoption of the spiritually lost. In his book *The Screwtape Letters,* C. S. Lewis imagined a conversation between two demons and he wrote (in the imaginary voice of a demon), "In the long run either Our Father [Satan] or the Enemy [God] will say 'Mine' of each thing that exists, and specifically of each man."[3] Satan, the great thief who comes to kill, steal, and destroy, seeks conquest over the image of God by destroying its bearers. Any child whom God redeems and brings into His family can never by claimed by the enemy. Satan is called the "accuser" (Revelation 12:10), and he is quick to point out the greatest obstacle separating humanity from God, namely our guilt. All humanity stands condemned as guilty before a just and righteous God and therefore can have no fellowship with Him: "For all have sinned and fall short of the glory of God" (Romans 3:23). That is why God sent Jesus. Our guilt was so overwhelming that Jesus would have to die and then rise again to atone for it: "For our sake he made him to be sin who knew no sin, so that in him we might become the righteousness of God" (2 Corinthians 5:21). Jesus came to bring lost children home and to see them adopted into God's forever family, but first they had to be redeemed: "But when the fullness of time had come, God sent forth

3 C. S. Lewis, *The Screwtape Letters: Annotated Edition* (New York: HarperOne, 2013), 127.

his Son, born of woman, born under the law, to *redeem* those who were under the law, so that we might receive *adoption* as sons" (Galatians 4:4–6, emphasis added). We were redeemed for a purpose, and that purpose was adoption. God does not just pay our debts; He invites us to sit at His table in His home as beloved children and makes us heirs of His immeasurable riches in Christ. He makes us "sons" enjoying all the rights and privileges of children belonging to a king.

Jesus came to redeem the lost but He faced overwhelming opposition to completing his redemptive mission. Shortly after His birth, Herod sent soldiers to destroy Jesus by commanding that every child under two years old in Bethlehem be killed. It was only by an angelic warning that Jesus and his parents made their escape to Egypt, where they awaited the end of Herod's reign. After His baptism Jesus was led out to the wilderness and, after fasting for forty days, was tempted three times by Satan himself. He met the challenge and, by the power of God's Word, sent Satan fleeing. In most places He visited, He was met by opposition from the religious elite, as well as from the unbelief of the people. At one point His own disciple, Peter, part of His inner circle, stood in His way as He set His face toward Jerusalem and the cross that awaited Him there. In the Garden of Gethsemane on the night before the crucifixion, Jesus bore the weight of the world on His shoulders, enduring stress so severe that it caused Him to sweat drops of blood. Throughout His entire life, and in each miserable step along the Via Dolorosa, Jesus faced unspeakable resistance to accomplishing His mission. Even death, that last and final enemy, when it sent Jesus to His grave, could not stop Him as He arose on the third and glorious day. At all points He prevailed, winning the marvelous victory over sin and death, and making a way of salvation and "sonship" to all who would believe. Praise God!

TRAVEL TO HAITI

I WAS STARING AT the computer screen looking for the best airline tickets. The time had finally come to choose a date, lock in the seats, and take off for Haiti to meet our boys. Anna and Grace would join Joelle and me as we made our first international flight. I hate flying. I fly when I need to because I understand the basic principles of aeronautics and because I have read all of the statistics showing that flying is the safest form of travel ever invented. In fact I read one statistic that claimed you have more chance of injury or death while sitting on your couch in your living room than you do on a commercial airliner. Intellectually I know that flying is safe. But despite that head knowledge, being stuck six miles up in the air inside what appears to be a giant toothpaste tube crammed next to two hundred other people traveling five hundred miles per hour just seems wrong. Flying may be safe, but for me it is not comfortable. I'm not sure if it is a fear of heights, claustrophobia, cramped seating, or bad food, but I do not enjoy being up there. By God's grace Haiti is not very far from the United States, and so our total air time would only be about eight hours. As I shopped for tickets, I saw again our computer screen wallpaper: the file photo of Wikelson and Richardson our agency had sent us. It was a sweet picture of them holding hands and looking up into the camera. I purchased the tickets, then looked those boys in the eyes and said, "We're coming for you little guys!"

My desire to meet my new sons overshadowed the discomfort of leaving home, but I still wanted to be prepared. After reading up on travel to Third World countries, I did my best to plan for the visit. The closest to international travel I had ever come was a visit to Victoria, British Columbia, when I was in junior high. That trip was with my parents and I don't think it should actually count. For my initial Third World experience I wanted to be armed to the teeth with everything I or my family might need. From the time I was a young boy, I was known as a "survivor," always being prepared for the worst, which sometimes meant sleeping with a machete-sized knife close at hand as I took the responsibility of guarding the entire basement of my childhood home from bad guys. With that part of my personality shining through, I stopped one evening on my way home from work at a Walgreens store to pick up some of the "essentials" on the travel list I had complied. I filled my cart with everything from sanitizing wipes, to anti-diarrheals (lots), to Pepto-Bismol (I bought every last box they had), to sleep aids, to pain medicine, to first aid kits, determined to be prepared for any scenario that might come up. I wish I had a picture of the clerk's face when I checked out and she said "Planning a trip?" as she scanned the eighth box of Pepto tablets. If she only knew that my shopping had just begun.

Next I moved to online stores, where I ordered water sanitation tablets—you know, in case there was another earthquake like in 2010 and we were stuck for weeks without clean water. Later that week at the sporting goods store, I found the rehydration salts I needed in case one of our crew became severely dehydrated. Before checking out I made sure to grab multiple bottles of industrial-strength mosquito repellant that may have been potent enough to kill a small horse. Then there were the "adventure wipes"—basically large diaper wipes made for bathing without water. My favorite part of that purchase was the strategic directions for washing your entire body with a single towelette. Suffice it to say, you should start at the top and work your way down! The last stop was to the pharmacy to pick up some heavy-duty antibiotics to have on hand if one of us contracted some nasty bacterial infection. When I finally had the chance to organize my loot and I saw it all in one place, I felt like a weird travel version of a "prepper," the kind of people who dig underground shelters in their backyard and collect canned food as they await the end of the world. With little care that I may have been becoming some kind of paranoid extremist, I happily stuffed my bags full and started the countdown to our departure date.

We left Portland, Oregon, on November 19, 2015, en route to Port-au-Prince, Haiti. After a brief layover in Atlanta, we boarded our final flight, scheduled to arrive right on time. As we made our way to our seats and crammed our bags into the overhead bins, we noticed right away that there would be empty seats on that flight, a welcome change from the overcrowded connecting flight from Portland. I took my seat next to a young black man, who I assumed must be Haitian, and noticed he was reading from a medical text book. As a medical provider myself, I saw this as an opportunity to start up a conversation and perhaps learn some travel tips before we touched down in Port-au-Prince. It turned out that he'd grown up in Haiti, but now lived in New York, where he was attending medical school. We visited briefly about the medical profession and then turned the conversation to the purpose of his visit to Haiti.

"This flight is normally full," he said, glancing around at all the empty seats. "Because of the limited number of flights from the US to Port-au-Prince, there are never any empty seats."

"Is that right?" I asked. "I guess we should be thankful that we found the one flight that is not packed?"

"No," he said, his tone changing slightly. "The reason the flight is not full is because of the political unrest in Haiti right now. There have been riots in downtown Port-au-Prince due to controversial elections. The only reason I am going is because it's my cousin's wedding and I already had the tickets purchased."

"Really?" I asked, trying to play it cool and not show any concern. "I hadn't heard about any unrest."

"Yeah, I grew up there and still have friends and family there, but I would not be going if it wasn't for this wedding. Is this your first time to Haiti?" he asked, obviously seeing me for the rookie that I was.

"Yes," I had to admit as I tried to show confidence.

"Well, Haiti is a wonderful place to visit, just not now. If you stay away from downtown, you should be fine."

Great, I thought. *Don't we have to go downtown for a meeting at the embassy? This man grew up in Haiti and even he doesn't feel comfortable traveling there at this time! What have we gotten ourselves into?*

Our conversation ended and I was thankful for the perspective he had given me on the situation there. I was also thankful that Joelle and the girls were sitting in a different part of the plane and did not hear any of our discussion. I did not want them to suffer any unnecessary additional anxiety. As my new friend and I turned our attention to our respective books and electronic devices, I couldn't help but notice a small knowing smile creeping across his face as he gently shook his head as if to say, "This guy has no idea what he is doing." That combination of a head wag and smile was something we would see often in our first hours in Port-au-Prince, causing us to wonder what inside joke we were clearly oblivious to.

Shortly after departing from Atlanta and for the next three hours, we bounced along as if we were traveling in the back of a covered wagon. I have flown enough to expect and not be alarmed by occasional turbulence, but this flight was rough from the takeoff to the landing. About one hour into the flight, the attendants handed out little green cards that had to be completed to pass through customs and immigration at the airport. I remember trying to fill it out but having difficulty writing because of the turbulent ride. For someone like me who doesn't care for flying anyway, the rough air added insult to injury. I felt in some small way like our flight was similar to the end of the movie *The Truman Show*. As you may recall, Truman was challenging the boundaries of his artificial life, the greatest of which was his fear of sailing. In order to discover and ultimately escape from this false reality, he had to overcome a formidable storm that had been created to discourage him from finding out the truth. The show's architect knew his weaknesses and tried to exploit them to the fullest, preventing him from moving forward. In the same way, my adversary knew my fears and weaknesses, and during that rough flight I could not help but wonder if a degree of spiritual warfare was at work, attempting to discourage me from moving forward. I do not want to make the mistake of attributing every difficulty in life or in our adoption process to spiritual warfare, but I think Christians probably err more on the side of under-recognizing, rather than over-recognizing, spiritual opposition. I don't know exactly why that flight was so turbulent, but if there was an opposing force that wanted to rattle my cage a bit, that was a good place to start.

Finally, after what seemed like a very long three hours, we began our descent and I looked out of the window to get a lay of the land. It was night, and to my surprise the city was, for the most part, completely dark with the exception of what looked like multiple large campfires dotting the streets. Any other major metropolitan area would be lit up like a Christmas tree, but not that place. Port-au-Prince was a city of millions of people and yet there was almost no light. As we drew closer to the airport, lightning flashes and pouring rain surrounded us. It was then I realized we were landing in the middle of a thunderstorm! The darkness I saw was not only because of the lack of utilities in the city, but the few homes that enjoyed electrical service must have had a power outage due to the storm. Thanks to the skill of the pilot, we landed without incident, and as I gathered my things and approached the cockpit, I overheard him explaining how he had navigated the aircraft in a trough between two thunderstorms throughout most of the flight. That would explain the constant bumps as we traveled. My prayer at that point was that God, like the pilot, would keep us safe, navigating us between the many storms that might threaten us over the two weeks that would follow. Joelle, Anna, Grace, and I stepped from the plane and into that dark city hoping to bring the light of God's love into the lives of little Wikelson and Richardson.

As we entered that foreign world, a wave of hot humidity poured over us like a steam shower. Unlike a thunderstorm in Oregon that tends to be cool, a thunderstorm in Haiti is warm and just creates more thick, steamy air. Even though we were there during the cooler part of the year, the heat and humidity were difficult to get used to. We passed easily enough through customs and immigration, our little green cards functioning exactly like they should. We did, however, elicit some giggles and head shaking from the airport staff just as I had seen when speaking to my neighbor on the plane. Since we did not speak French or Creole, we were not part of the inside humor that was apparently enjoyed at our expense. Perhaps the locals thought we were unwise to be visiting their country during elections, or maybe I just had some of my lunch still smeared across my face—either way we were good entertainment.

We collected our baggage (thankfully it had all arrived) and headed outside to try to find our driver. That was the one part of the visit I had been particularly concerned about. Have you ever been to the circus and seen the amazing acrobats on the trapeze? As they fly through the air "with the greatest of ease," there is a point at which one acrobat lets go of his handle, and if he does not catch the hands of the acrobat on the approaching trapeze, he will fall a fearsome distance to (hopefully) the net below. Well, up to this point in our travels, we had been holding fast to our trapeze, getting to where we needed to be and catching the flights that we had scheduled. Now that we had arrived in Haiti, we had to let go of any control we thought we had, set foot in a strange land, and hope that someone was there to catch us lest we find ourselves in a free fall. One of my fears as the leader of our mission, with my wife and two daughters following me, was to be stuck at the Port-au-Prince airport looking for a driver who never showed up. I did not speak the language, I did not know whom to trust, and I did not know if I would be able to reach anyone at our agency or at the guest house where we would be staying.

"Thank you Lord!" I whispered when I saw a young man standing in the doorway that led outside and holding a cardboard sign that read *"Garland family."* The other trapeze had showed up, and we grabbed hold of those waiting hands with a firm and thankful grip. We followed him outside and attempted unsuccessfully to hop over the large puddles (Anna describes them as small rivers) that covered the breezeway walk that led to the parking area, our shoes and pant cuffs becoming soaked with water. After fending off several aggressive "red shirt" cab drivers fighting for our business, we found the van that would take us on the thirty-minute drive to the BRESMA guest house, loaded our luggage in the back, and headed out into the dark and stormy night.

I had hoped that, following our bumpy flight, the turbulence was over, but then I had never traveled the roads of a Third World country at night in a thunderous downpour. While I was thankful to have my now wet feet on the ground again, I soon found out that another small adventure stood between us and the guest house. The streets of Port-au-Prince at night in the middle of a thunderstorm are not somewhere I would choose to spend any length of time. On that night, however, those streets stood between us and our final destination. We had climbed into a van with a driver who did not speak English, at least not to us, and trusted him completely with our lives that evening. *I really hope this is our guy* was the prevailing thought in my head as we started out into the night. My concerns slowly turned to confidence as I watched him navigate through a maze of tortuous and extremely rough roads. It was disorienting driving through the city because of the walls. We were used to driving in residential and business areas back home in Oregon where you can see the actual homes, businesses, yards, landscaping, and other building features that help give a sense of where you are. If you live on a residential street, imagine what your neighborhood would look like if each home was surrounded by a ten-foot cement wall. Instead of looking over at your neighbor's house and seeing the new paint on the siding, or the flowers in the pots on the front porch, or even the weeds in the front yard, all you would see is a large, drab wall. If each home was surrounded by a wall, and each wall was connected to the one adjacent to it, your appealing neighborhood street would be transformed into a narrow, boxed-in corridor. If you can now imagine winding and steep roads, filled with hairpin turns, all boxed in by these cement walls, you have a good idea of what driving in Port-au-Prince is like. It is the city version of a corn maze, and just as confusing.

As it turns out, the storm drains we see along the city streets in the United States actually serve a purpose, and that purpose is to keep the roadways from becoming waterways during a heavy rain. In Port-au-Prince the storm drains were either missing or dysfunctional, because we plowed through what seemed like class one or two rapids as the rainwater freely flowed down the steep streets. Because much of the city is built on a hillside, the roads make fast-moving rivers during a storm. At several low points between two hills, we encountered small ponds where water had collected and overflowed, following the path of least resistance. The driver handled all these obstacles with ease, listening to talk radio, and looking as relaxed as a commuter in an American suburb on the way to work. If he did not seem concerned at all about the conditions, then maybe neither should I, I figured. As my dad is fond of saying, "It was an opportunity to trust," and trust is what we did.

We arrived safely at the guest house, a small, castle-like compound complete with a wall, gate, and guard. Two honks of our driver summoned the gatekeeper to let us inside, a welcome refuge indeed. Those two staccato honks, "Beep-beep," would become a comforting and anticipated sound during our visit, indicating that our driver had come for us, wherever we may have been, to bring us back to the safe haven that the guest house had become. That sound was also special because it was the password required to open the gate at the orphanage, granting us access to meet and spend time with our sweet little guys. It's funny what sticks with you after returning home from a trip like that, but those two honks ended up being something I looked forward to hearing again as we waited for our return visit to Haiti. It would be those beeps that, as we waited outside the large gate, opened the door to the final chapter of the adoption, when we entered BRESMA for the last time and brought those boys home.

We enjoyed a beautiful evening meal prepared by the guest house staff, who had waited up extra late for our arrival. Bedtime is typically early in Haiti and we did not realize the accommodation in the schedule they had made for us until we learned the daily routine over the remainder of our stay. Typically dinner would be served between 4:00 and 5:00 p.m., but that night they waited until after 9:00 p.m. to serve us, and we were glad they did. Following our meal, we settled into our rooms and took a collective deep breath, thankful that we had arrived and that within twenty-four hours we would be meeting our sons. Before going to bed I crept down the stairs to meet the nice man with the shotgun who sat all night by the front door and offered him some American junk food in the form of Oreo cookies. He was the night guard and I wanted him to like me, and what better way was there to do that than by giving him cookies? He accepted the gift with a friendly smile and grateful handshake. I had a sober appreciation for our guard, because each evening he would carefully search the courtyard for intruders while providing a staunch deterrent as he pumped the shotgun cocking it with a loud "chh-chh." That sound would certainly make anybody think twice before climbing the wall! Being worn out from our day of travel, I headed back upstairs and drifted off to sleep, listening to the sounds of that foreign city as they echoed in the dark just beyond the razor wire atop our fortress wall.

FIRST MEETINGS

OUR FIRST MEETINGS with Wikelson and Richardson were at the same time very ordinary and very extraordinary. There were no green meadows at sunset, filled with blooming wildflowers and flitting butterflies, in which we ran into their arms for a joyous first embrace. There was not even an official ceremony in which we waited on pins and needles as the orphanage staff prepared the boys and then presented them to us for the first time as our (soon to be) new sons. In fact there was not even a translator, or anyone for that matter, who spoke enough English to properly introduce us to them. For an uninformed observer, this day might have seemed somewhat routine because of the lack of any fanfare or sign that something special was about to occur. There were no balloons, streamers, cakes, or treats, but this day was special, because a miracle was about to take place.

It was November 20, 2015. I was feeling mostly excited but also a little nervous that morning, so I did not eat much breakfast at the guest house. Brimming with anticipation, we all loaded into the van, our bags packed with photo albums, toys, and treats for the boys. After a ten-minute drive we pulled up to what appeared to be a large house surrounded by a concrete wall with a heavy-duty ten-foot metal gate protecting its entrance. I have to admit that the gate was intimidating, topped with multiple arches, each one featuring sharp spires to discourage uninvited visitors. The orphanage sat tucked back along a steep and narrow street surrounded by homes, some of which were heavily damaged (by the earthquake of 2010, I assumed) and undergoing repairs. The bumpy driveway down to the gate was a dramatic descent from the main road, so much so that it would be easily missed by an unfamiliar driver. The first time we took that sharp turn down to the orphanage, I thought we would plummet into a ditch!

As we waited at the gate, two quick honks of the van horn signaled the gatekeeper, who slowly slid open that impressive barrier to reveal a large and colorfully painted multi-story building, all of its doors and windows protected by decorative bars. The name of the orphanage was Brebis de Saint Michel de l'Attalaye, and for obvious reasons it was often abbreviated as BRESMA. We sat nervously in the van, trying to contain our emotions, and looked for directions on what to do next. I think we may have been expecting a presentation similar to the opening scene of *The Lion King*, in which the new baby king, Simba, is presented to the animals on the savannah in spectacular fashion, lifted high above the watching crowds as they cheered for and adored him. For us there was no such production. On the contrary, after waiting for instructions, one of the staff members looked at us, seemingly bewildered that we were not doing anything. He motioned us to the front door, as if to say, "Don't you want to go in? Go in and meet your boys!" So that's what we did. With little direction or guidance, we entered that four-story building, explored it on our own, and tried to identify the two newest members of our family. We must have looked a little lost, because some of the staff would gesture in the general direction we should be heading to provide us with clues along the way as if we were playing a game of hot-and-cold. I could almost hear their voices saying, "Warmer...warmer," as we got closer to finding the boys.

First we found little Richardson, just finishing the last few bites of his breakfast that was being fed to him by one of the nannies as he stood near her, dressed in a T-shirt and diaper. That particular floor was home to the two- and three-years-olds. All of the boys had their hair buzzed short, and they were all approximately the same size, each in various stages of eating breakfast. On the menu that particular morning was a large plate of cornmeal for each child. It took a little searching, but when we found Richardson, we slowly approached him to say hello for the first time. As Joelle put her hand on his back and knelt down beside him, he gave her the look of a three-year-old boy who was mostly interested in cleaning his plate by devouring every last bit of breakfast that it held. We learned throughout the rest of our time that food is a hot commodity for the kids there and not something to be wasted but cherished, down to the last grain of rice or noodle on a plate. Seeing that he was preoccupied, we each gave him a little hug, careful not to interrupt the path of the spoon on its way from the plate to his waiting mouth, and moved on to see if we could find Wikelson.

We followed the hall from Richardson's room down a narrow corridor and up a flight of stairs that led outside, where we carefully stepped past a group of young girls playing what appeared to be jacks. That game was different, though, because instead of metal jacks and a ball, they were using small rocks. We took a moment to say "Bonjou" (Haitian Creole is most similar to speaking French), and then made a tight hairpin turn to the left, finding a door that opened into a large room filled with tables, benches, and about a dozen children watching television. The eyes of the children wandered slowly from ours to a flight of stairs across the room as we searched for Wikelson, looking intently at each face. Noticing their glances to the stairs, we turned to see one of the bravest little boys I have ever met, courageously walking down the steps to meet his new parents. Approaching slowly, he took one moment to greet us with his deep brown eyes, and then, without saying a word, a look of hopeful acceptance spread across his face and he fell into a warm embrace from one happy mama. Then he took Joelle's hand and headed for the stairs. He had something to show us. I was following a few steps behind, and not wanting me to feel left out, Wikelson turned and, with a happy but solemn expression, reached an open hand back to me as if to say, "Come on, Papa. I want you with us too." I have heard it said that 80 percent of communication is nonverbal, and during the two weeks we spent with Wikelson and Richardson, we spoke very little, but communicated very much. Without a doubt they knew they were valued and loved, and we knew that we were accepted.

We were led to a small room upstairs on the top floor of the building that was filled with little boys and girls about the same size as Wikelson. We did not fully understand what was happening at the time, but after watching that moment later on video, we discovered that he was proud of us and wanted us to meet all of his roommates. He had led us by the hand to his special living area to present us to his friends as his new papa and mama. Of course it was an honor for us to meet his friends, to hear their names spoken in his voice, and to hug each one. We were so thankful that he had a group of close-knit "brothers" and "sisters" to play with, eat with, sleep with, share with, and cry with. That was a special time indeed, but Wikelson was not done. We had not *all* been together yet. Taking us again by the hands, he led us back downstairs to find his brother Richardson, probably not realizing that we had already met him. That was Wikelson. He was always taking care to look out for and share with those around him—a quality that was easy to fall in love with.

We found Richardson a happy boy, his tummy full of breakfast, with newly brushed hair, fresh baby powder on his neck, and a clean set of clothes on his back. With misty eyes and thankful hearts, Joelle and I held those boys, relishing our first moment together as parents and children. We looked forward to the day when all eight members of our family could be together as one.

On the surface this meeting may have seemed like a special or sweet occasion as two children were introduced to new parents who would one day take them home. On one level that day was both special and sweet, but it was so much more. A profound mystery was being revealed, one that had been kept hidden since before the foundation of the world. The mystery is that God had intended, before time began, for these exact children at this exact time to join us as a part of our family according to the counsel of His great will: "In him we have obtained an inheritance, having been predestined according to the purpose of him who works *all things* according to the counsel of his will…" (Ephesians 1:11, emphasis added). Paul also taught us in Ephesians 1:4–5 that God "chose us in [Jesus] before the foundation of the world…[and] predestined us for adoption to himself as sons through Jesus Christ." This incredible passage says that God chose us, those who would believe in His Son, before we chose Him. Just as God, by the purpose and counsel of His will, looked forward in time and chose me for adoption as a "son" into His family, so He planned with all wisdom and foreknowledge the entrance of Wikelson and Richardson into our family. That meeting day was no ordinary day; it was the culmination of God's perfect plan.

When Joelle and I were married eighteen years ago, we never saw that day coming, but God did. He had worked everything out to achieve His grand purpose and now we were watching that purpose play out right before our eyes. Just as it is surreal to think that God predestined me as a son, it was surreal to recognize that I was a part of God's plan for these fatherless boys. His providential hand was just as much at work in the choosing of Wikelson and Richardson for our family as it was in knitting together our four precious biological children in the womb. Our adoption is but a faint picture of a deeper reality—the overwhelming love that God has for His children, and the foresight He shows by placing the lost into homes, both on earth and in heaven.

"WE HAVE A PROBLEM."

Very early on in the application process, our agency director told us to expect problems to pop up in the course of the adoption. Haitian adoptions were notorious for taking a long time to finalize because of the many unforeseen obstacles that prevented forward progress. During one email exchange with our director, Joelle had expressed some concern about a possible crack developing in the adoption over a question of the relationship between the boys and their biological mother. In response to the concern over this small crack, the director wrote, "Lady, you do not want to know the gaping holes of possibility that underlie each and every international adoption. Each one is a legal and procedural miracle." That reality check helped us to appreciate the tenuous nature of international adoption, and we were thankful that we had yet to see any major setbacks. It also made us very aware that a setback was likely on the horizon and that it was more a matter of "when" rather than "if" it would occur.

The administrative offices for the BRESMA orphanage were located at the guest house where we stayed. It was reassuring to see all the comings and goings of the staff, because we realized how diligently they were working to get all the kids into homes. It was also frustrating because they were the only people we met who spoke English, and because they were so busy they had little time for any questions that were not "business related." We arrived at the guest house after our first meeting with the boys, still basking in the warmth of that joyous moment. After finishing our lunch we headed upstairs to relax for the afternoon. The staff was very careful to respect our privacy, only venturing upstairs to call us for meals, so we were surprised when the maid came and told us that the director would like to speak with us. Not being sure of what would happen next, we made our way downstairs to the administrative section in the house and stepped into her office. We walked into that busy room in which an overhead fan gently circulated the warm air. Behind a large desk covered in a variety of computer accessories and paperwork stood the orphanage director with two files, one in each hand. After a brief greeting we sat in the two chairs opposite her desk, and I felt a lump pop up in my throat when she said matter-of-factly, "We have a problem."

Here we go, I thought. *I knew this was all happening too easy. Maybe she will ask us for more money?* (I had heard of that sort of thing happening in other international adoptions.) *Maybe there is a major health problem with one of the boys? Now that we've come all this way and met them, how can we turn back now? How could we be so foolish to think this would all work out? If there was a "problem," why didn't they find it before we traveled all the way here?*

In the few seconds that passed after I found out that "We have a problem," my mind covered the gamut of negative possibilities that statement implied. As Joelle and I sat there bracing for the worst, the director broke the news by saying, "You don't eat bread." She paused for a moment and then continued, "I spoke to the maid this morning and she told me you did not eat much of your breakfast at all and you did not eat any bread."

I will always remember the wave of relief that washed over me at that moment. The problem was with our eating habits, not with our adoption process, and that I could handle. She continued by saying, "You will be staying with us for two weeks and we need to know what you like to eat." We were then able to explain to her that because I was nervous and excited about meeting the boys, I had no appetite that morning, and Joelle is gluten intolerant and so she never eats bread. We agreed on some other breakfast fare for the remainder of our stay and left her office being very thankful that food was our problem that day.

OUR DAYS AT BRESMA

IN TOTAL WE spent parts of nine days with Wikelson and Richardson. We were not allowed to see them on the weekends, and during the weekdays we were limited to four to five hours of visiting time. Each morning we would awake at the guest house to the sounds and smells of a Haitian breakfast being prepared. We enjoyed a spread that usually boasted many tropical fruits, delicious pancakes, omelets, pastries, and hot dogs (yes, hot dogs). Shortly after our meal we would gather our things and the driver would arrive to take us on the ten-minute jaunt from the guest house to the orphanage. I really enjoyed that drive. I always felt surprised at how busy the streets were early in the morning, with an abundance of pedestrian and motorized traffic. Street vendors hiked along the roadways, hauling their goods to the best spots for a day of sales. Tap-taps (buses or trucks used as shared taxis) packed to the brim with people on the way to work and children on the way to school navigated the congested intersections. Motorcycles sped by with little regard for life or limb weaving in and out of traffic. The prevailing rule of the road in Haiti seemed to be "Ready or not, here I come!" rather than the "Yield to the driver on your right, yield to oncoming traffic, yield for pedestrians, etc." that is expected in the United States. At first it seemed like this almost reckless driving style would get us all killed, but I came to appreciate it as a wonderful and complex dance in which cars, motorcycles, tap-taps, and pedestrians all worked together to avoid catastrophe. Pretty much everyone was going to "go," and if you weren't ready, it could spell trouble. Needless to say, we made it safely to the orphanage each day and enjoyed getting better acquainted with the our sons.

Wikelson and Richardson did not speak English, but there was one Haitian phrase they used that we learned very early, and the sound of it brought joy to our hearts. Shortly after our first meeting, they (especially Wikelson) began calling us "Papa Blan" and "Mama Blan." Of course we knew what "Papa" and "Mama" meant and that in itself was special, but it took us a day or two to interpret the descriptor "blan." When we finally found out they were calling us "White Papa" and "White Mama," we thought it very endearing. There was not a hint of negative racial overtone, just a plain statement of fact with no pretense or prejudice, said as casually as my son Daniel calls me "Daddy." Needless to say, these boys did not interact with white people very often, and their acceptance of us despite our physical differences was very touching.

As I was accepted into their lives as a papa, I was reminded of my heavenly Father. They called me "Papa" because of horizontal human adoption just like I call the Father "Papa" because of vertical divine adoption. By the process of adoption, our relationships were changed and both of us were granted a privilege that we previously lacked—access to a father. Mine was a lack of a spiritual Father and theirs was a lack of a human father. My prayer was that one day they would be adopted for the second time, and that it would be an adoption into the family of God as His children.

⁓

Our days at the orphanage were filled with coloring, reading books, listening to music (Wikelson loved "God Is Enough" by Lecrae), playing, snuggling, and just hanging out—with Anna and Grace enjoying and making the most of their time with their soon-to-be new brothers and the rest of the kids.

At first Richardson would not say a word and would insist on being held close the entire visit, but toward the end of our time, when he became more comfortable, we saw his personality breaking through. Whether it was throwing his brother's things across the courtyard or running back to his "homeroom" to share dried fruit and nuts (they called it "candy") with his friends, we saw a rambunctious and caring little boy coming out of his shell.

For me, the sharing at the orphanage was the most unexpected and inspiring characteristic of the kids who lived there. With few exceptions the children, both younger and older, would share their treats with those around them, even if it was something very small. It was not just Wikelson and Richardson, but most of the kids we interacted with had this attitude. It was as if they knew what it was like to be hungry, the gnawing stomach pain and loss of strength, and they never wanted any one of their friends to experience that feeling. It is unfortunate that it takes an impoverished orphanage setting to nurture the virtue of sharing, but it may be one of the only silver linings for the plight of the kids who lived there.

We had been told to expect an erratic meal schedule during our visit. We would not be eating with the kids at BRESMA, and so our midday mealtime was at the mercy of whenever our driver showed up to take us back to the guest house. In preparation for that, I purchased several large bags of Costco trail mix and separated them into snack-size portions in small plastic baggies. I figured the combination of dried fruit and nuts would hold up well to the heat and not spoil during our fourteen days in Haiti. Of course, each time we reached into our packs to sneak a little bite, all eyes were on us, especially the eyes of Wikelson and Richardson. It was fun to share the nuts with them and see their faces twist up into puzzled expressions as they tasted the new textures and flavors for the first time. Walnuts were particularly disconcerting to Wikelson, but with some mild prompting he would furrow his brow in determination and swallow them down. The dried fruit was the biggest hit. The kids called it "siret" ("candy") in Creole. When the "candy" bag came out, little Richardson would lean in and reach for it with the single-minded fervor of a boy with a hungry tummy. He had developed a taste for the raisins—to him a rare jewel mixed in among the nuts. That is why it touched our hearts one day when Wikelson, aware of his brother's love for them, grabbed a bag of trail mix and began picking out all of the raisins. At first I thought he was sorting out the good stuff in the same way my kids at home liked to pick out and eat all the marshmallows from their Lucky Charms cereal (usually provided by the grandparents). But instead of tossing the handful of raisins into his mouth, he reached over to the waiting hand of Richardson and ever so slowly dumped the treasure, taking special care not to spill any of them. Delighted with his gift, Richardson sat and ate with a satisfied look on his face. Wikelson had placed the needs and wants of another above his own, and that was an example I hoped to follow as I let go of my own selfish desires in serving my family.

∾

In an orphanage you are forced to grow up fast, but Richardson liked being a baby, and who could blame him? One of the saddest things about orphans in Haiti, or anywhere else, is that they often take on roles that exceed their number of years. Instead of playing make-believe house, a little girl may actually need to take care of younger siblings in the way a mother would, robbing her of her childhood innocence and replacing it with responsibility. At the time of our visit, Richardson had just celebrated his third birthday, but at times he seemed to contest this new "grown-up age" in the same way a thirty-nine-year-old woman may contest her fortieth birthday. By the way he pressed his little face against my chest as I held him, or by the fact that he would not let us put him down much of the time, he clung to his babyhood. We observed one funny episode where a seven- or eight-year-old girl, who was not that much bigger than he was, picked up Richardson and then proceeded to bounce him on her hip and make little "Sh-sh-sh" baby noises as if she might be rocking a newborn to sleep. That loving attention was reassuring to us, knowing that, even if his mother was not there, he still got much-needed hugs. For the first several days of our visit, we did not even know if he could talk because he was so quiet, using mostly gestures to get what he wanted. Unfortunately for him there were times when playing the role of baby just wasn't cutting it and he had to show his true big boy self (which we were delighted to see).

One of these times happened during lunch. As I mentioned previously, mealtimes were special, and in particular, they were special to Richardson. On several days the nannies were busy with all the other children, and we got assigned to help Richardson with his lunch. One of the first things we noticed about him was that the nannies would spoon-feed him his meals. As you may recall, that is what was happening when we first met him. This seemed sort of sweet, but also out of place, because most three-year-olds should be feeding themselves. Joelle was off playing with some of the older kids, and I was left with Richardson and a large plate of noodles. I began feeding him the best I could as he sat on my lap. My left arm was wrapped around his little body, securing him in place next to me and holding the plate of food, and my right arm was doing the work with the spoon to feed that hungry boy. About halfway into the meal, Richardson grabbed the spoon from my hand and began shoveling the noodles into his open mouth. Apparently I was not scooping bites of food large enough or fast enough. That little boy enjoyed being treated as a baby, but there were certain times that he had to take matters into his own hands (literally) and fend for himself. I was somewhat conflicted by Richardson's baby ways because, on one hand, I wanted him to experience all the nurturing love that is critical to the development of a young boy, but on the other hand, I did not want his development to be delayed in an unhealthy way. When in doubt, it is always better to err on the side of too many hugs rather than too few, and the fact that Richardson was getting the attention he seemed to crave warmed my questioning heart.

~

This book is full of pictures in the form of earthly events reflecting heavenly realities. Many of these pictures are beautiful, as they image the glory of God and His unfathomable love for His children. If one was to imagine actual paintings that image God, they would be filled with intricate detail and engaging color as only the most gifted artist could create. It is not only in fine art, however, that God reveals Himself, but sometimes He uses even the simplest drawings to illustrate a precious truth. Such was the case when I, mustering all of my artistic talent, was drawing stick figures on a small erasable white board with Wikelson. It was a quiet and warm morning. Wikelson and I were hanging out on a set of stairs that descended into a welcoming tile-laden courtyard that featured a large shade tree bursting forth from a centrally located planter. Those decorative yellow and orange concrete steps had become a favorite spot for reading, coloring, and just sitting together. The special moment came when I began to draw a stick-figure family like the ones often seen as window stickers on cars with each member of the family represented. Similar to the car stickers, my drawings included parents that were bigger and children that were smaller, appropriately decreasing in size according to their ages, and sometimes I even added in a pet for good measure. As I drew the members of our family (all eight of us) Wikelson's countenance became bright as he realized what was happening. He was represented as a member of our family! While we could not speak much with words, that simple stick-figure family was speaking volumes to him. With a satisfied smile and giddy excitement, he would ask me to draw each member of the family over and over, including Mama Blan, sisters blan, Richardson, and he was always sure to include Emma and Daniel, whom he had not yet met but had seen in photos. Even Kavik, our red-coated Siberian husky who waited for us back home, was often added in to make the family complete. To see the peace on Wikelson's face as I connected my stick-figure hand to his was a moment I will cherish forever. Finally this little guy knew that he had a family, and in his thorough enjoyment of those drawings, he demonstrated that knowledge in no uncertain terms. He and Richardson were a part of us and we were a part of them and that had become clear with a simple stick-person demonstration. While there were many special moments during our visits, that one really stood out because of the meaning behind it. We were actually communicating on a deep level, and it was all because of pictures. Those humble representations taught a profound truth: a new family unit was being formed. Perhaps that is why God uses so many pictures in our lives to show us Himself. He knew long before the colloquial phrase had become popularized that a "picture is worth a thousand words." For Wikelson and me, a thousand words would have fallen far short of describing the beauty of that morning together.

If a picture is worth a thousand words, how much is seeing the first smile on the face of your son worth? Most parents experience that blessed moment when their baby begins to become more expressive and, looking up into adoring eyes, offers a vague upward curl of the lips, sparking celebration over a first smile. Those times can be confusing, however, because perhaps your baby is smiling at you or maybe he just has gas—it can be hard to tell. One of the advantages of meeting your new son when he is already three years old is that when he smiles at you for the first time, there is no doubt about it.

Because of the warm weather in Haiti, we were always sure to have plenty of water bottles in our daypacks to prevent dehydration. It was the first day of meeting the boys and I had not yet become used to the heat. Sitting down on a blue metal-slatted bench, I reached for my water and settled in for a little break. Richardson, who may have been motivated by his own thirst or maybe just a desire to get a closer look at me, approached with a solemn expression on his face. Standing just to the left of me with his hand placed gently on the armrest of the bench, he lifted up his eyes to meet mine. In what seemed like an unplanned staring contest, our eyes remained locked for the better part of a minute. That's when it happened. The clouds parted, the sun broke through, and the warmth of Richardson's smile shone on my heart. That ray of light disappeared just as quickly as it had come, and after a small sip of water from my bottle, he went on his way, leaving me to enjoy replaying that moment in my mind.

It is important to understand that even though Richardson had a smile that would melt the hardest heart, he did not overuse it. In fact, after viewing some of the photos from our visit, our agency director commented that she had never seen Richardson smile before in any of her previous visits to BRESMA. That precious smile was a rarity and, like all rare things, its scarcity only increased its value. To see it was to find a hidden treasure sparkling in this little boy's otherwise sober demeanor. Richardson soaked up our love like a dry sponge in need of water, and most of our time with him was spent just sitting and cuddling. He seemed to be a serious boy who was reflecting on what all this newness around him could mean. The more time we spent together, the more often we enjoyed seeing his smile as his personality began to break out during game time, tickle time, and when throwing his older brother's toys. We looked forward to the day when we could enjoy that smile in our own home—in Richardson's own home—on the day we finally welcomed him officially into his new family.

～

One of the primary virtues that I witnessed at BRESMA was bravery. We saw many instances of bravery demonstrated during our visits, because although these kids lived in a crowd, they were still all alone. The nannies that worked there were amazing, showing love and giving attention to the kids whenever possible, but they were not the same as having parents. We witnessed everyday trials, like the falling and scraping of a knee, or being hungry, or just being lonely, met with courage that children should never have to show.

Toward the end of one day, as we were gathering our things to head back to the guest house, we noticed that Wikelson was nowhere to be found. We realized that it was getting close to lunchtime and we figured that he had run upstairs to eat. I didn't want to leave without saying good-bye and so I climbed the stairs to the large room where he normally ate with the other kids his age. What I found at the top of the stairs will not soon be forgotten, because there sat Wikelson by himself, absently stirring a plate of food, with large tears streaming down his face. He knew we were leaving and that made him sad, a show of emotion that we had not yet seen from him. I sat down on the little plastic chair next to him and put my hand on his back, trying desperately to provide comfort. It was times like those that I wished I spoke Creole and I could reassure him of my love. We sat together in silence for a moment, and then he turned his head and with tear-filled eyes looked at me and then toward the door and said, "Ale" (Ah-lee). I did not need Creole lessons to learn what that meant; the knife in my gut said it all. He was telling me to go. "You want me to ale?" I asked as I pointed to the door.

"Wi," he said while nodding as he tried to compose himself, sniffing softly and holding back the tears. Wrapping my arms around his shoulders, I pulled him in close for a hug. Then I looked him in the eyes and told him I would be back in the morning before I finally started the long walk down the stairs and out the door to the van waiting outside. I left behind a five-year-old boy whose soul was much older than that, having had to develop coping mechanisms for all the loss experienced in his short life. I was proud of him for the bravery he showed that day because he did not want me to leave but he knew it was necessary. I also hurt for him because no young child should have to carry the heavy burden of sending his father away, not knowing for sure if he would ever return.

Leaving Wikelson that day was difficult, but on the way back to our temporary home at the guest house, I saw something that helped to ease the pain. The afternoon traffic seemed particularly heavy as we made our way slowly through town. While we were waiting in a line of cars at one of the few intersections that actually had a stoplight (more of a suggestion than a rule), a motorcycle glided by on our right, dodged between a couple of slow-moving cars, merged effortlessly with the flow of traffic, and headed off out of sight. That a motorcycle had passed us was not unique or surprising in any way; in fact it was routine in the course of traveling the streets of Port-au-Prince. What surprised me was the young boy, probably just a bit older than Wikelson, sitting on the back, his arms wrapped gently around the driver, and his face relaxed in one of the most serene expressions I could have imagined. Despite all the bustle around him it was as if he were sitting on a couch reading quietly with his mother or resting contently after a satisfying meal. As the motorcycle made its way through the traffic, he had no fear or anxiety on his face but instead a contented peace that I admit I felt jealous of. His hands were not gripped in white-knuckle panic, but rather held on just enough to keep his balance as his body swayed smoothly, perfectly matching the bike's rhythm. While I do not know for sure, I like to imagine that the boy was traveling with his father that day, and that he had complete trust about where he was going and how he would get there. Because of his faith in his father, the boy was at rest, without a care in the world.

God spoke to me through that scene. My desire was to be just like that boy, holding fast to my Father, and enjoying a perfect peace on the road He had willed me to travel with Him. Though I was frustrated and saddened by leaving Wikelson behind, I had to remind myself that this was ultimately God's story and that he had a plan in place. Even the hard times during the adoption process would be filtered through His hands and would be useful to accomplish His purpose in us and in the lives of Richardson and Wikelson. I prayed quietly in the van that God would grant both me and Wikelson the peace that I saw on the face of that young motorcycle passenger—the peace that passes all understanding: "Do not be anxious for anything, but in everything by prayer and supplication with thanksgiving let your requests be made known to God. And the peace of God, which surpasses all understanding, will guard your hearts and your minds in Christ Jesus" (Philippians 4:6–7).

ADOPTION IN A BROKEN WORLD

The Lord is near to the brokenhearted
and saves the crushed in spirit.
PSALM 34:18

HEARTS WERE NEVER meant to be broken. In love, God created us for a joyous and eternal fellowship. But now we live in these broken times looking back to what once was and looking forward to what will be. As Christians we can be assured of our adoption in Christ. Because of our union with Him we will one day enjoy all the riches of heaven and an inheritance of life. But for now, with the entire creation, "we...groan inwardly as we wait eagerly for adoption as sons, the redemption of our bodies" (Romans 8:23). Our adoption into God's family is certain because of the finished work of Jesus Christ, and we have already received the Spirit by which we can cry out "Abba Father," but we await the consummation of our adoption—that is, the final victory over the very presence of sin, the redemption of our physical bodies, and the restoration of the creation. We live in the "what is" somewhere between the "what was" and the "what will be." During this time we wait with an eager sense of hope, knowing that our Father is coming for us.

The same was true for Wikelson and Richardson. Their new family had come to provide them with a loving home. They were wanted, valued, and cared for. No more could they be considered fatherless, because by the grace of God a father had come to claim them as his own. That was a wonderful, but painful reality. The same wonder that is present upon the first day of life, when a baby is welcomed into the world by the awe-filled arms of loving parents, was present when we met Wikelson and Richardson. These were our sons—and the day we met them was every bit as special as the birthdays of our biological children. But because of the drawn-out and convoluted process known as international adoption, they could not yet come home, a painful reality breaking their hearts and ours. The birth of a baby is wonderful thing, but what if the parents had to wait months to bring the precious little one home after meeting him or her for the first time? That would dampen the joy of that first meeting, wouldn't it? The two weeks we spent with Wikelson and Richardson were priceless, seeing the joy on their faces as we arrived each day. But it was also painful, seeing the tears in their eyes each time we said good-bye. After each visiting day we left them with hugs and kisses and reminders that we would come back the next day. But ever looming was the final good-bye when we would leave and not return the next day, or the next day, or the day after that. Sure, we knew that one day we would return for them, but how could the innocent minds of a five-year-old and three-year-old, who had already suffered the loss of their father and mother, process that truth in a meaningful way? Like the Christian waiting for his final redemption, these boys were now caught in the in-between times, waiting in hope for the consummation of their adoption. They were no longer orphans, but at the same time they were not yet home. "For in this hope we were saved. Now hope that is seen is not hope. For who hopes for what he sees? But if we hope for what we do not see, we wait for it with patience" (Romans 8:24–25). Wikelson and Richardson could not see or even imagine their new earthly home, and yet they waited for it with hope and patience. It is that same hope and patience that is present in believers looking forward to their heavenly home.

It is ironic that our process of drawing the fatherless near was filled with so much separation. Our deep desire was to provide a home for those boys, but the socialization visit felt more like a cruel joke instead of a step closer to our goal. We had met and fallen in love with Richardson and Wikelson, and for the first time in their two years living at the orphanage, they had parents. Just when our hearts had become knit to theirs, it was time to leave, ripping apart those newly thrown stitches. We left Haiti incomplete, as part of our family stayed behind. The pain that we felt from being so close to them and yet so far away is still real to me today.

The final good-bye was a heart-wrenching challenge. Wikelson seemed to understand that we would return someday and he was looking forward to flying with us in an airplane to our new home. What he was not aware of was just how far off that someday might be. Just like any other child, his concept of time, especially when it came to future events, was very limited. When we tried to explain that it would be a long time until we returned, he assumed that meant a day or two. The concept of a six- to twelve-month wait is not easily comprehended by a small boy, and despite our best efforts he thought we would all be together again soon. Because of that hope the reality of us leaving probably did not sink in until we did not return for several days. For him our final good-bye was said with a feeling of optimism in anticipation of a coming reunion. It still breaks my heart to imagine the confusion and sadness that he must have experienced as he waited day after day for us to come back. I prayed that God would comfort him and that he would not have to cry himself to sleep at night as he dealt with those all too familiar feelings of abandonment once more. Perhaps the stories of other children finally getting to go home with their parents would calm his anxious mind as he waited for his turn. Whatever the case would be, we left him in the hands of a more than capable God who could comfort even the most saddened of souls.

Unlike Wikelson, Richardson was not so optimistic. Even at his age of three years old, he had the sense that something was wrong. To put it simply, he did not want us to leave. Richardson was our baby, and babies do not do patience well. When there is a need to be met, they need it met right away. Richardson's need was the love of parents and in particular the tender warmth of a mother's arms. In our family we talk about filling each child's emotional cup with love to the point where they are full and satisfied. Richardson's little cup had been filled during our visit, but unfortunately the love cup has a hole in the bottom and it must be poured into daily to remain full. It was as if he knew that this new source of love was disappearing, because he clung desperately to Joelle and me as we left for the final time. Because Joelle was struggling to fight back her own tears, the lot fell to me to carry Richardson to his room and say the last good-bye. That was a particularly hard task because it meant prying his little hands from my own, putting him down among a crowd of other toddlers, and turning my back to him as I walked out the door. As we entered the small room where he ate his meals, the room where we first met, I was hoping to find one of the nannies in order to hand him off to her so that she would be able to comfort him. To my disappointment nobody was available, and so I had no choice but to put him down and hug him tight, telling him that I loved him and that I would come back for him—a message that was drowned out by the sobs of a broken little heart. One of the hardest things I have had to do was to stand up and walk away from Richardson that day. It felt so wrong to just leave him there, but I had no choice. The driver was waiting and I had to go. So I turned and with heavy feet started toward the door. Trying to ignore the sounds of a crying child pleading for me to stay, I stepped into the hall and disappeared.

The following day was December 3, 2015, and we traveled home to Oregon uneventfully and tried to get back into a normal routine. The highlight of arriving at home was the hugs and smiles we received from Emma and Daniel, who had been spending a fun-filled two weeks with their grandparents while we were away. Being separated from them for so long was difficult, but it brought much needed refreshment to our souls to see them again as we returned from Haiti with heavy hearts. We had missed a traditional American Thanksgiving and so we had some catching up to do on holiday spirit with Christmas just a few weeks away. We traded in our flip-flops, sandals, and shorts for warm hats, gloves, and scarves, and though we tried to enjoy the cheer of the season, it was hard because we missed our little guys so much that it hurt. I am normally "Mr. Christmas" in our home, rivaling Chevy Chase in the movie *Christmas Vacation* with my zeal for every tradition that the season brings. That year, things were different. Of course we still celebrated, but there was something missing. Or maybe it was somebodies who were missing. It may have been that no one other than Joelle, Anna, Grace, and me noticed, but there were empty seats around our table that year—seats that should have been filled by Wikelson and Richardson. Despite the absence of our two newest members, I was not without hope. because I envisioned the blessed occasion that, by God's will, we would all be together celebrating the birth of Jesus for the first time as a family of eight in 2016!

We did some email debriefing with our agency, sending them pictures of our visit and checking in on the status of our paperwork. It was discouraging to learn that the time-line from the end of our socialization visit to the expected return trip to bring the boys home would be eleven to twelve months! While I had heard that figure before, it had not really sunk in completely. Now that we were facing that wait with the knowledge of who Wikelson and Richardson were, it seemed like an eternity. How could we press on through another year of that slog? We prayed. We prayed often and we asked others to pray. And God, because He is faithful, comforted our hearts, wiped our tear-filled eyes, and gave us the courage to take one day at a time as we waited on his perfect plan. This was the seemingly endless "in between time"—the time between what was and what will be. It was a difficult time for us as adoptive parents, just as it is for us as Christians as we await the consumma-tion of our vertical adoption. In both instances God gave us and gives us everything we need to press on each step of the way. All we could do was wait and hope that things would move along more quickly than we had expected.

IN THE MEANTIME

"THE PREPONDERANCE OF THE EVIDENCE ..."

W<small>E LOVED THE</small> fact that Wikelson and Richardson were brothers biologically. As we considered adopting two children versus one child, we decided overwhelmingly that it would be better to bring a sibling pair into our home. Trying to put ourselves in their shoes, we felt that it would be reassuring and comforting for them to look across the dinner table and see a blood brother (or sister) with the same background, experience, and roots. Even orphans who are adopted into a loving family may continue to feel isolated because they are different from everyone else in the home. But what if they were not alone? What if there was someone else in the household who had the same fears, doubts, and questions? Our hope was that having a special part of their biological heritage would help take some of the pain away from the loss suffered by all orphans who miss their first families.

You can imagine our distress when we received a letter from the US Embassy just a few months after returning home from Haiti stating that "The preponderance of the evidence" was not satisfactory to establish their family relationship. Not only was this disappointing because we wanted them to have that special bond, but it also put the entire adoption at risk. If these kids had been presented to the orphanage as brothers, but in fact they were not, then we did not truly know their identities and therefore they would not be eligible for adoption. There are many criteria that must be met prior to the approval for a child to be adoptable in Haiti, and of course a proper understanding of who they are and where they came from is paramount for the safety of everyone involved.

The solution was to perform a DNA test. Fortunately labs in the United States offer DNA testing to determine family relationships, and all we had to do was contact one of those and have a kit sent to Port-au-Prince to collect the samples. After a week or two, we would have the results and that would be that. Either the adoption would move forward without skipping a beat or it might be over because of potential fraud. There is no doubt I was shaken by that development. One of our biggest concerns throughout the entire process was that we would be adopting children who actually needed to be adopted without any shady dealings or questionable histories. The last thing we wanted was to be involved in an unethical adoption. What was it about their paperwork that failed to convince the authorities of their relationship as family? Had we and our agency missed some glaring inconsistency in their history? How had we come this far only to be one test away from them being declared unadoptable?

About one month after we first sent the test kit to Haiti, we received the results. The words in that letter make me chuckle a little each time I go back and read them. I think it is partly joy and partly incredulity that makes me laugh, because the letter said that based upon a DNA match greater than 99.99 percent, the boys were 30,677 times more likely to be full biological brothers than not. It is amusing to me that based on those results the lab would not just say it like it was: they were brothers, 100 percent, without a doubt. Suffice it to say that the officials who questioned the boys' relationship were satisfied with the new "preponderance of the evidence" that showed Wikelson and Richardson came from the same family by 30,677-to-1 odds. With those test results, once again God provided a little piece of evidence that He was the Author of this story and that we were following His lead.

"THE ONES WITH THE SHAVED HEADS!"

Obviously Wikelson and Richardson stand out in our family photos because of their beautiful deep brown skin. One of our primary concerns in adopting them was the prejudice we might encounter for being a mixed-race family. How would we be able to preserve their culture and heritage in a meaningful way as they were raised in a white family in the predominately white Pacific Northwest? I still do not have all the answers to those important questions but I want to share a brief conversation that shows the refreshing perspective of a child. An exchange between my four-year-old nephew Rainer and his mom helped to ease my mind a bit about the acceptance of the boys into our family as well as our culture.

It started with my sister-in-law Grace saying, "We haven't seen Emma and Daniel in a long time!"

To which Rainer replied, "You know who we have never seen? Our cousins!"

Unsure of whom he meant by "cousins," Grace answered, "You mean Ben and Kathleen (Joelle's sister's kids)?"

"No," Rainer said. "The other cousins. The ones with the shaved heads!"

"Oh, you mean Wikelson and Richardson."

"Yeah, we've never seen them yet!"

I could only smile—"The ones with the shaved heads!" Rainer had seen many pictures of Wikelson and Richardson before they arrived home with us. It would seem that the only distinguishing feature he noticed was their short hairstyle and nothing else. It was not their skin that set them apart but their haircuts. We knew that at times skin color would be an issue for our boys, but we prayed that most people would have the eyes of a four-year-old boy who just saw them as kids like himself—except with short hair!

"NEVER LET YOUR FINGERPRINTS EXPIRE!"

Shortly after the DNA test we encountered a new challenge. Believe it or not, the Department of Homeland Security and the FBI are involved in international adoptions. That is because adoption creates new citizens of the United

States and the goal is to make that a lawful process. As part of the initial screening of potential adoptive parents, there are multiple background checks at the state and federal level to ensure that criminals are not being approved to adopt. In addition to screening the parents, efforts to prevent child trafficking include screening procedures for the children as well. On the federal level potential parents and adopted children must be granted clearance by the US Citizenship and Immigration Services (USCIS, a division of Homeland Security). As with any thorough background check, the USCIS requires fingerprinting as a part of their investigation, and the FBI is responsible for clearing the prints by cross-checking them against their criminal databases. For a person with no criminal background, that is not a complicated process. It is, however, a slow process usually taking about six weeks to complete.

Because my closest brushes with the law consisted only of a few minor traffic violations, I had no concern about being cleared and I was not surprised when my record came back clean on the initial screening. But there was a catch. The background check is only good for six months before it must be completed again. An adoption that lasted several years would require multiple updates to the USCIS file. Just because the initial screening was good, who's to say that a potential parent wouldn't have some indiscretions later on making him unfit to adopt? To show USCIS that we continued to be law-abiding citizens, we were careful to update our file every six months. To allow time for the paperwork to clear, we would submit it about

eight weeks prior to the expiration date. If our fingerprints expired at any point during the adoption process,
it could lead to long delays and other problems that we
did not need or want. It could mean going back to square
one with USCIS and erasing all the work that had been
done over the previous several years. At this point you are
probably thinking that it should be simple to just go to the
local USCIS office and redo some fingerprints, but that is
not the case at all. It is a convoluted and complicated process that I will not even attempt to explain here. That was
why our agency stressed repeatedly, "Never let your fingerprints expire!"

It was Wednesday, May 18, 2016. We were rejoicing to be
months ahead of schedule on bringing the boys home. Our
supposed twelve-month wait had been cut nearly in half. If
the pace continued, we would be traveling to Haiti in July or
August to finalize the adoption, and that sounded so much
better than December. The marathon we had been running
appeared to be coming to an end, and we felt as if the finish
line was nearly in view. My fingerprints were set to expire in
August and so Joelle called USCIS to start the paperwork to
renew my file. What she found out when speaking to one of
the agents was troubling to say the least. She was informed
that her own file had not been updated from the previous
six months and was set to expire on May 27, just nine days
later. Despite our submission of the paperwork six weeks
earlier, Joelle's file had been neglected. Remember that it
was very important that our prints did not expire and that it
normally took about six weeks to renew them. With that in

mind nine days seemed like the blink of an eye. We needed her file updated immediately and that meant we needed multiple departments of the federal government to move at light speed. In other words we needed a miracle.

After multiple attempts Joelle was able to reach a real live person at the USCIS application center. Her request for an explanation and a plan of action were met by stiff resistance from the officer working on our case. "This is the FBI we are dealing with," the woman said. "I will submit your paperwork, but there is no expediting the process!" Essentially we were told to go back to the end of the line and restart the six-week application.

After learning the discouraging news, Joelle promptly called our agency to figure out what to do. Unfortunately our agency did not have any additional pull with the bureaucracy than we did, and we were directed to call our state senator's office for help. To me that suggestion seemed like it would get us nowhere. It is what you say when you have a gripe that no one else wants to hear: "Call your senator!" In my estimation a senator's office was the place that all complaints go to die because they fall only on deaf ears. Why would my senator, whom I did not vote for by the way, care at all about our adoption troubles? I am pleased to say that my estimation was incorrect, because instead of being ignored or brushed aside, Joelle was able to speak with a helpful staff member who became an advocate for us in completing our paperwork.

Each attempt by Joelle to call USCIS and all email correspondence were met by a stonewall reply: "Your file has been submitted for processing." While that was positive, it was unacceptable. Her file had to be completed right away to avoid major problems and delays. We needed an expedited approval because they were at fault for not processing our file weeks ago when it was first submitted. By that time there was a weekend upon us and we knew nothing would happen outside of normal business hours, so we waited anxiously for Monday to arrive. At our small group Bible study Sunday evening, we prayed with our friends that God would move in an amazing way. He had answered so many of our prayers and provided so faithfully during our journey that we approached Him with confidence that He would act. I have to admit that early on in the adoption process, I was a little surprised by direct answers to our prayers, once again showing the defects in my faith. In that situation, however, I had a profound peace because I knew that God had brought us that far and that He would see us through to the end.

"YOU NEED TO UNDERSTAND THAT THIS NEVER HAPPENS."

On Wednesday, May 23, Joelle received a direct phone call from the same USCIS agent who had been so dismissive of her initial requests and complaints. Her demeanor had completely changed from annoyance at our audacity to ask for an expedited process to a pleasant disbelief as she reported the good news of our approval. "First of all, you need to understand that this never happens," she said in an agreeable tone totally foreign to the previous interactions. The agent went on to explain that not only was the FBI able to clear Joelle's prints, but they were emailing a confirmation letter as a downloadable file so that we would not have to wait for it in the mail. According to her, emailing a letter was an exception she had never before witnessed, and she seemed a little stunned that it was being allowed. When the call ended, Joelle checked the email and there was the letter just as promised. Overjoyed, she called our senator's office to thank that specific staff member who had been so helpful. As it turned out, just a few hours earlier, they had placed a call to the FBI to advocate on our behalf. When Joelle told them the good news, even they seemed shocked to hear that the file had been completed. It was as if they had been happy to help, but they really did not believe it would change anything. It seemed that the approval surprised nearly everyone involved in the process—except God, that is. He had that situation under control before it ever came up. With one more hurdle behind us, we pressed on to the finish line that was now just a few steps ahead.

COMING HOME

I will not leave you as orphans; I will come to you.
JOHN 14:18

HOW DO YOU explain the unexplainable or describe
the indescribable? How can you ever know the unknow-
able? Some things must be experienced to be known. Even
our imaginations, as creative as they may be, are limited
to a certain extent by our experiences. In other words
our imaginary thoughts tend to build upon things we are
already familiar with rather than inventing completely
new concepts. If there was a wonderful land that you had
never visited but only heard about through fleeting whis-
pers and faint images, how could you know what that
place was like except by going there? What if that place
was your new home—your real home—and what if you
had inklings that it was better than anything you could

ever imagine? What if it was a place that you knew you would someday go, but you did not know when? Wikelson, Richardson, and I could all relate to this longing for a new and better home. Their transition from orphans in Haiti to a family in the United States and all the joys and comforts that came along with it mirrored my eventual transition from this very damaged and imperfect world to my heavenly home. Just as they looked forward to a place they could not really imagine...so do I.

How do you tell a child what playing on grass is like when they have never done it before? Imagine the questions he would have as you described this green plant that grows like a shag carpet, covering the soft soil and creating a cool and refreshing surface. For a child who has known only concrete floors and an occasional patch of dirt, what would it be like to run barefoot for the first time across a lush green lawn? What would it be like to roll down a soft grassy hill? How could you explain those experiences with words, especially with the sorts of words a child's mind could comprehend? As I said, some things in life you just have to experience personally to understand what they are like, and playing in the grass is one of them. I asked Daniel what it is like to play in the grass and he said, "It is like flying like a bird." Enough said. You just have to do it.

What about the gravity-defying sensation of a park swing? The feeling that now, as an adult, makes me nauseated was a thrill like no other as a child. I remember the wind in my face, the weightless gliding through the air, and the attempts I made at flying as I jumped from the swing at its highest forward point, landing in a heap of exhilarated laughter. How was I to describe the swings at our home to Wikelson and Richardson who, as far as I could tell, had never experienced one before? How could I teach them to pump their legs, propelling the swing higher and faster, without actually sitting them down in the seat? Who could understand the fun of Dad running underneath the swing as he pushed with a mighty underdog (or, as my kids like to call it, an "under hotdog") unless you had actually experienced it? When I asked Emma what it was like to swing, she answered simply, "It is really fun!" It was hard for her to describe except to say that it was amazing. You just kind of have to do it to get it.

What does ice cream taste like on a warm summer day? The sweet, creamy goodness of licking a scoop of chocolate followed by the crunchy fun of eating the cone cannot be imagined. It must be experienced to be appreciated. If the boys had ever tasted the joy of ice cream at BRESMA, those times had been few and far between. How overwhelming would it be to walk into a place like Baskin-Robbins and see more flavors than you ever thought possible of a food that you never knew existed?

What about jumping on a trampoline, riding a bike, going to the zoo, sleeping on a pillow in your own bed, having plenty of food every day, or speeding down a slide at the park? How about enjoying the feeling of a warm bath or shower? That is an extravagance that Wikelson and Richardson never knew at the orphanage, and yet they would experience it almost daily in their new home.

What is this magical place where all of these things are readily available? In what kind of life are these luxuries so abundant that they become rather commonplace? As I write these words, I am convicted of my own "taking for granted" of the many privileges I enjoy living in America. I understand that material blessings are not my sole source of joy and comfort in this life and there are many in the world who live with much less than I have who are happier than me. It is a mistake, however, to not give thanks to God for His abundant provision or to downplay all the blessings that have been bestowed upon our country. My hope was to use some of those blessings to bless others who are less fortunate.

At this point it is important to say that Americans are not better than Haitians. There are many aspects of Haitian life and culture that we as Americans would do well to learn from. Just because Wikelson and Richardson would soon live in the United States, it did not mean their lives would be easy. We would be bringing them to a place where they would experience racism the likes of which they would have never known in their native country. Not only would they have to deal with discrimination from whites, but even some in the African American community may not fully accept them because they belong to a white family.

Americans are certainly not better than Haitians because of our wealth. Haiti was not always a poor nation—at one point in its history being known as the "Pearl of the Antilles" because of its beauty and richness. In the same way, the United States may not always be a rich nation, but for now we have been blessed with the resources to come alongside children in need and share the goodness we now enjoy with them. My purpose is to use the blessings in my life to help those who are struggling, not to judge one people group as better than another simply because our circumstances differ. I could have just as easily been born in Port-au-Prince as I was in Portland. The fact that God has placed me at this time and in this location is for His purposes, and I want to serve Him well because, "Everyone to whom much was given, of him much will be required, and from him to whom they entrusted much, they will demand the more" (Luke 12:48).

Along those same lines I have heard some criticize the use of horizontal adoption as a picture of God's rescuing spiritually lost children. That criticism is based upon the perceived elevation of adoptive parents to a "God-like" status and the diminishment of orphans to a "sinner-like" status. From that objection it would appear that adoptive parents, particularly those who live in a wealthy country like the United States, are placing themselves inappropriately in the role of a "savior" while seeing orphans as the only ones in need of saving. While I can sympathize with these sentiments, I believe they are misguided. Pictures are images—they are not the real thing. I am commanded to love Joelle just as Christ loves the church, but my loving her in that way does not imply that I am Christ and that she is the church. Our relationship is an image of something greater, and that image is not meant to be taken to its extreme interpretation. Adopting a child no more makes me God than loving my wife makes me Jesus. Just because our adoption serves as a picture or reminder of God's love, it does not elevate me or diminish Wikelson or Richardson. I am not better than they are. They are just as capable of imaging the love of God as I am, and I watched them do that very thing on several occasions when they gave sacrificially to share with their friends.

The more I reflect on the adoption of Wikelson and Richardson, the more I am reminded of my own adoption. Rather than viewing myself in the position of God in rescuing the helpless, I have realized more deeply that *I am* Wikelson and *I am* Richardson. My spiritually helpless state was just like their physically helpless state: we both needed a home. We were all in need of a sort of rescue. Of course I began writing this story about two orphan boys in Haiti, but I am continually being drawn to the similarities I share with them and the greatness of God for being the Author of their adoption story as well as my own. Adoption is not just the story of two boys from Haiti finding a new home. Adoption is my story as a lost child being reconciled back to his loving heavenly Father.

With those things in mind, let's turn our attention back to the anticipation of the boys coming home. It was fun for me to think about Wikelson and Richardson experiencing all the good things that their new life would offer them. In the months leading up to their arrival, I would often spend time looking out the window into our backyard and dreaming of them running, playing, and jumping with the careless joy all children should know. As we prepared their room, I couldn't wait to tuck them into the beds specially made for them. When we ate meals together as a family, two empty chairs sat ready and waiting for the newest members to sit down and join us. As the days grew closer to their arrival, we had fun filling their dresser with new clothes for them to wear. We had sought them out and now we had prepared for them a place, and we waited on the edge of our seats to finally welcome them into their new home so they could experience it firsthand.

Isn't that a wonderful picture of God the Father as He waits to welcome His children into their forever home with Him in heaven? Jesus said, "In My Father's house are many dwelling places; if it were not so, I would have told you; for I go to prepare a place for you. If I go and prepare a place for you, I will come again and receive you to Myself, that where I am, there you may be also" (John 14:2–3 nasb). As a Christian, how am I supposed to imagine heaven? I can try, but this broken world is all I have ever known—my experience can only take me so far and even my imagination is limited by a finite human capacity. When it comes to my eternal home, I cannot even comprehend the word *eternal* let alone all the good things that have been prepared for me there. There are good things to be enjoyed in this life, but even the very best things on this earth will pale in comparison to the mundane (if there is such a thing) things in heaven. Living in the United States in a stable family situation is better than living in Haiti as an orphan; however, living in heaven in the presence of our "Abba Father" is infinitely better than any life on this earth. Wikelson, Richardson, and I have all looked forward to a better life; for them it was living in a family, and for me it is living in heaven. Their hopes were fulfilled when they each became a Garland, but my hope has to wait for now. My prayer was that one day they would join me in waiting for that ultimate hope as they too are "seized by the power of a great affection"[4] of God the Father. My desire was not just to bring them into my earthly home, but to point them toward their heavenly home, which would be infinitely better. The most important relationship we could ever have would not be as father and sons but as brothers in Christ, forever worshipping together before the throne of God.

Children coming home is a precious thing. At the memorial service for my sweet 103-year-old grandma, one of my dad's childhood friends, Paul Holmes, gave the message. The Scripture that he used was Psalm 116:15, which says, "Precious in the sight of the Lord is the death of his saints." While death is certainly our enemy and it will be conquered at the return of Jesus, the writer of Psalm 116 describes it as "precious." How can this be so? Well, when we think of it in terms of a child of God finally coming home to the beautiful place that has been prepared for her, it is precious indeed. To imagine my grandma, a follower of Christ who left behind a legacy of faith, being welcomed home is a precious thought even though it required her death. God loves to see His children coming home, and I am convinced that He looks forward to the day that

---

4 Brennan Manning, *The Ragamuffin Gospel* (Colorado Springs, CO: Multnomah, 2005), 195. It should be noted that, although Manning is often credited as the author of this creative phrase, he actually attributes it to the Deep South from many years ago and how it was used in the same fashion as "born again" is today.

He has planned when *all* of His followers will be present together with Him. I had a small taste of that anticipation as I waited for Wikelson and Richardson to come home. These were my children, but they were not yet home because we were separated by time and distance. How precious would it be when at last they arrived? Although it would not take the pain of death to see us united, the pain of losing their parents and the painful process of adoption serve as a reminder of the difficulties in bringing children home. Jesus said that, "... It is your Father's good pleasure to give you the kingdom" (Luke 12:32). Our heavenly Father takes great pleasure in preparing for us and giving to us an eternal home in His kingdom. Following His example, it was my absolute pleasure to give a part of my earthly kingdom to Wikelson and Richardson by inviting them to join my family.

THE ARRIVAL

*Like cold water to a thirsty soul, so is
good news from a far country.*
PROVERBS 25:25

I REMEMBER IT CLEARLY. We were at a gas station when we heard the good news. It was a gorgeous day in the San Juan Islands—a little piece of heaven tucked away in northwest Washington, sandwiched between the United States mainland and the Canadian border. After the first night of a four-day family camping trip, Joelle, Anna, Grace, and I left our larger group and went to town to fill up the tank and pick up some supplies at the grocery store. Being from Oregon, I was not used to pumping my own gas. We are one of only two states, joined by New Jersey, where the common people are not entrusted with that responsibility. I was outside the car working the pump, and I felt a small sense of accomplishment that I'd completed the task without starting a fire or causing an explosion, proving the regulators of my home state sorely mistaken. Feeling my confidence growing, I moved on to try my hand at washing the front windshield, and that is when I noticed that Joelle was using her phone. Of course that was nothing out of the ordinary, and because we did not have cell service at the campsite, I figured she was taking that opportunity to catch up on messages or maybe check her Facebook page. I finished the last swipe of the squeegee, barely leaving a streak, and climbed back into the driver's seat to head out for the store.

"We're cleared," Joelle said with an excited but measured tone. "I just got the email from USCIS and we're cleared."

After waiting 236 days from the last time we saw the boys and 1,229 days from when we started the adoption process, the final approval from the United States Citizenship and Immigration Services had been completed. Indeed that was good news from a far country, and it meant that within a couple weeks we would be traveling to Haiti to finally complete our journey. It was a surreal moment for both Joelle and me. Rather than bursting out crying, or laughing, or celebrating, we just sort of sat there in a state of... well, shock, I guess. When you have been waiting for the light through an indefinite night, you are rightly stunned to see the first rays of sun break through the shadows. It had been dark for so long that we had begun to lose hope of the dawn. Just like eyes adjusting to the morning day, our emotions took a few minutes to adjust to this new reality. For all intents and purposes we were done. All that remained was to book our tickets and go get Wikelson and Richardson and bring them home. The seemingly endless paperwork, fees, and bureaucracy of the adoption process were actually coming to an end. The sense of relief that the heavy burden of waiting had been lifted from my shoulders was quickly overcome by a sense of responsibility for those two lives. They were our children now. They had no one else. They were ours and they were counting on us whether they knew it or not. In some ways the journey was nearly over, but in a more profound way than we could ever know, the journey was just beginning.

There is a very small airport on Orcas Island where we were camping. Joelle has a mother's heart, and I believe sincerely that if she could have convinced one of the pilots to fly her to Port-au-Prince that very day, we would have left just hours after getting that email from USCIS. Never mind that all the aircraft were small prop planes used for tours: her kids were in an orphanage and they needed a mama—right now! As it turned out, it would be a couple weeks before we could actually leave due to some logistical issues both at home and in Haiti, so we enjoyed the remainder of our camping and then headed home to make all the final preparations for the arrival.

The lead-up to that trip was completely different compared to our first visit to Haiti. Rather than fear and anxiety, I was filled with excitement and peace. I have never run a marathon before, and I hope that I am never stricken with the desire to try. I can imagine, however, that when a runner who has covered 26 of 26.2 miles sees the finish line ahead, he gets a burst of adrenaline that helps to propel him to the end of that grueling event. I think I was enjoying a kind of "runner's high" as the conclusion of the adoption approached, and I rode that all the way to our travel date on August 17, 2016.

Because our flight was scheduled to depart at 6:00 a.m., we left our house at 4:00 a.m., and as we pulled from the driveway in those wee morning hours, it occurred to me that the next time I saw our home, our family would be dramatically different. We left that day a family of six, and in just few days we would return (Lord willing) a family of eight. And it was not merely numbers that we were adding, but two little hearts who had fears, troubles, and doubts that most certainly would become our fears, troubles, and doubts in the coming days, weeks, and years. As already discussed, adoption is a process that involves pain, and our family was about to experience that firsthand. Of course, not all pain is negative. In many cases some pain is necessary to achieve a worthwhile goal, and my conviction was that God wanted me on this path and He would see me, Joelle, our biological kids, and our adopted kids through even the most difficult times ahead.

The day we left Wikelson at BRESMA in December 2015, he was talking about going with us to ride on the "avyon." He would move his little hand across the sky, making his best airplane impression as his eyes looked hopefully into mine. It killed me to leave him there, and I hoped he would remember our plans to fly to a new home when we finally returned nine months later. We arrived in Haiti on a hot and sticky mid-August night. After a brief visit to the US embassy in the morning to pick up some final paperwork, we headed out for BRESMA. As we pulled up to the large gate, I was struck with a similar feeling to what I had when I left our home a day earlier. I knew that this would likely be the last time we would see the BRESMA orphanage, and as we would leave there with Wikelson and Richardson, their lives would never be the same. That was a pivot point, a watershed moment in all of our lives, as we moved from what once was to what will be. It was a landmark moment that will always be remembered.

Unlike our first visit, this time there was no mystery surrounding what kids were ours or where they could be found. We knew exactly where to go. I followed Joelle up to the third floor, where we found Wikelson in his room. His nannies were preparing him to leave, and he had never been more ready to go. Because we were not sure if the boys would remember us or if they would be scared to leave with us, we planned an extra day in Haiti so we wouldn't need to drag them from the orphanage kicking and screaming. If necessary we could get reacquainted with them on the first day and then return the second day to take them home. As it turned out, that precaution was not needed, because it was not five minutes after embracing Joelle and me that Wikelson took our hands and headed for the door. He wanted to gather up Richardson and get on the avyon—right now! He picked up exactly where we left off as if it was yesterday, which was an answer to many prayers over the months of waiting.

Heading downstairs, we found what we affectionately called "the minion room," where the two- and three-year-olds lived. Immediately upon entering that place, you are surround by a swarm of little bouncing minions with their short and squishy arms extended upward, each vying for attention and love. As we approached, Richardson was quickly whisked away by one of the nannies. It was not to hide him that he was taken, but to prepare him. The nannies really seemed to care for Richardson, and they did not want him to go without first getting a fresh pair of clothes and a quick wash. Needless to say, when we did get our arms around that little guy, it was a sweet reunion. Like his older brother, Richardson seemed to remember us well and had no trouble showing his infectious smile and treating us to giggles, hugs, and kisses. As was usual for him, Wikelson watched us loving Richardson with the satisfaction of a proud father. He really enjoyed when his brother was taken care of, and the look on his face seemed to be one of excitement, not just for himself, but also for Richardson, who would at last have a real home.

With Wikelson leading and no time to waste, we walked outside, where the driver had just arrived to drop off some visitors. Wikelson saw the van and wanted to leave, and so that is what we did. In less than one hour from first walking in the door, we were gone, and in what we now recognize as normal for Haitian culture, there was little formality or fanfare. We just said a quick good-bye to anyone nearby as we all piled together into the small van. At our church we cannot even pick up our kids from the nursery without presenting an identification number. After all we had been through, I was not one to complain about a lack of paperwork, but it did seem odd that there was no official checkout process, papers to sign, or ceremonies to complete at the actual orphanage. All of that had been taken care of previously, so we just walked in, grabbed the boys, and walked out as proud parents. They had nothing to bring except the clothes on their backs. There were no special toys, pictures, or memoirs from their first family—it was just them. They were two brave little boys who were leaving everything they had known for the past two and a half years to begin a new life with a new family in a new home. They were Garlands now. Their names had been officially changed a few months earlier, but that day seemed like the consummation of their new identities as they left the old behind and stepped into a new world. We took them home to the guest house, where we spent the afternoon trying to stay cool and just enjoy being together.

I do not want to belabor the point that Wikelson was looking forward to the "avyon," but at about 5:00 in the afternoon that day, he wanted everyone to go into the bedroom. He lay down on the bed, and so we just figured that he wanted to take a nap. After all, it had been a big day for him and he was probably emotionally drained. To our surprise he wanted all of us to climb into our beds, pull the covers up, and turn the light off. Apparently Wikelson was ready for bed and we would all be joining him. We questioned what he was doing, and after several attempts using our limited Creole, we were able to figure out that he wanted everyone to go to sleep because he thought we were leaving in the morning. In his mind the sooner we all turned in for the night, the sooner the morning would come and we could fly away together. It was challenging but we were able to explain to him that it would be two "sleeps" before we left. Once that message got through to him, bedtime was over. The covers flew off, the lights came on, and it was time to play again.

Richardson just took everything in stride. As long as his brother and his mama were close by, he remained a content boy. Remove either one, however, and the tears were sure to follow. He did everything well during our first days together. He ate well. He slept well. He played well. And he seemed to adjust to Mama and Papa very well. One of the highlights of our first hours together was showing Richardson the new clothes we had brought for him. His face lit up with pure joy and excitement as he was presented a new pair of flip-flops and some shorts with matching shirts. The best part was the sweatshirt with a warm hood to combat the air-conditioning he was about to experience for the first time in the guest house, air-ports, and his new home. He and his brother had probably never owned any sort of jacket before, and so that was a special occasion. We were filled with happiness as Richardson removed his old clothes, setting them to the side, and warmly embraced his new outfit with a smile that is hard to put into words. It was a first of many firsts that would follow in the days and weeks to come. We did not want to rush Richardson to cast off his old "orphanage clothes," because that was part of who he was. Those items were some of the last strings that connected him to his orphanage home for the last two years, and we wanted to be extra careful not to tear them away too quickly. Our caution was met by his exuberance as he quickly slipped into his new clothes with a proud expression on his face.

The putting on of new clothes was a symbolic time as well. That occasion was a beautiful parallel to Ephesians 4, where Paul admonished his readers "to put off your old self, which belongs to your former manner of life and is corrupt through deceitful desires, and to be renewed in the spirit of your minds, and to put on the new self, created after the likeness of God in true righteousness and holiness" (Ephesians 4:22–24). As a Christian, a child of God the Father, I am to put away the things associated with my old life and embrace the identity that is mine in Christ Jesus. I am to identify with my new life instead of with my old life. In order to move forward in my Christian walk, some aspects of myself must necessarily be left behind. In joining God's family I have no option to continue wearing my old clothes. I have been made new—and that newness means leaving the old behind.

Unlike the way Paul described the old self, I would not call Richardson's old clothes corrupt or deceitful; there was nothing wrong with them. The nannies had taken care to be sure he was one of the best-dressed boys on his big day of leaving with his parents. My point is not that his clothes were somehow inferior to what we had provided for him, but only that putting them off served as a symbol of moving into new life. The clothes themselves were not really the issue. It was what the changing of clothes pointed to that was important, namely the leaving of one life for another. To fully join our family, Richardson could no more cling to his old life than I could cling to mine as I accepted Christ and grew in my faith. The changing of his physical clothes, while unnecessary on some levels, was a powerful reminder of what happened the day we brought him home. He was a part of us now, and that transition was not only occurring in his heart as he grew to love and trust us, but also in his appearance as we dressed him as one of our own. While we would be sure to hold on to those orphanage clothes as a memoir of his past and a part of his life we would never hide from him, he could no more continue in that previous life than a Christian could continue in his.

We spent our "extra day" at a local hotel that featured a beautiful swimming pool. It was fun to see the boys enjoy the water, and it was a perfect place to avoid the heat throughout that day of waiting. Wikelson quickly found some children who spoke Creole and began to proudly explain to them that I was his papa, which brought giggles and looks of disbelief to their faces. When they came to me to confirm his story, I did my best with my rudimentary Creole to tell them that he was my "petite gason" (little man) and I indeed was his papa. The fact that he would claim me as his own in a public place one day after leaving BRESMA—and do so with a look of pride in his eyes—was a touching moment for Joelle and me. He was "all in" when it came to his new family and was not ashamed to say so.

When it came to traveling, Wikelson and Richardson seemed like seasoned professionals. The ease with which they handled the lines, crowds, sights, and sounds was quite impressive. We began our journey home early in the morning on August 20. We moved quickly through the airport lines in Port-au-Prince. In fact we were treated like VIPs. The moment we pulled up to the curb, one of the "airport staff" ushered us through the check-in process as if we were celebrities. He first asked if we were a part of an adoption, and when I answered, "Wi," he directed me to follow him. Somehow he convinced the Delta airline staff that we were priority members, even though we were not, allowing us to skip the long line for boarding passes and baggage checks. Next he led us to the front of a formidable line that had piled up at the entrance to the security checkpoint. The security personnel had not yet arrived, so the line was not even moving. Our special guide marched us right past all those who had been waiting, removed the boundary rope that contained everyone in their places, and positioned us as the very first in line.

My suspicion began to grow when another "helper" came up to me and asked if he could put in a good word for me so that we would make it through immigrations without delay. "Give me $20 and you have no problem, okay?" he said in broken English and standing well within the boundaries of my personal bubble. Call me naïve, but I figured out at that point what was happening. I had just bribed my way through all the hassle of the airport, and now, just like feeding one pigeon is sure to bring all their friends in for a snack, I was surrounded by several men with their hands out eager to speed things along for us. I had tipped the first gentleman for assisting us through the check-in line, and because of my lack of negotiating skills and my lack of small bills, it was a good tip of $20. Obviously that was enough to make me a target for a quick buck. Because they'd kept asking if we were adopting and they always wanted to see my adoption paperwork, I assumed what was happening was normal and I was a little afraid to decline their directions. Once I got my bearings and realized what was going on, I found my backbone and told the last couple "assistants" to leave us alone. My hope was that they would not then sabotage our progress. After all, they had aided us, so could they not also hurt us? I was glad that they let us keep our privileged place in the security line, and to be honest, I was glad to have greased the wheels with a little financial oil. As far as I was concerned, avoiding the long lines standing in a stuffy and sticky airport was well worth the money I paid for that luxury, but I did not want to be taken advantage nor did I want to work the system. We had our paperwork in order and I was not concerned that there would be any issues with immigrations, and fortunately there were none. We flowed easily through the rest of the airport and, to Wikelson's delight, stepped on to the "avyon" right on time.

We had three flights to complete before we were home and overall it was a very pleasant day of travel. As we made our final descent into the Portland airport, I sat back and watched, admittedly with a little mist in my eyes, as the boys crowded the window, each vying for the best view of the beautiful Pacific Northwest. First we saw the majestic Cascade Mountain range, followed by the foothills covered in evergreen woods. Next came breathtaking views of the mighty Columbia River Gorge to the north and the scenic farmland of the Willamette Valley to the south. As we drew closer to the metro area, Wikelson was thrilled to see homes come into view, and he wanted me to point out his new house. "Gade (Look), Richardson!" he would yell over and over as he excitedly pointed to the new world below. I mentioned before that I do not enjoy flying; however, the final twenty minutes of that flight is time I will cherish, not only because it was the end to a very long journey, but also because of the pure joy I saw in their faces and heard in their voices as they reveled in the first sight of their new homeland. The air was smooth that evening and we gently descended, following the course of the Columbia River, the runway coming into view, as it always does in Portland, just as it seemed we would land in the water. We made a perfect touchdown and that was it. We were home.

Throughout the entirety of the adoption process, we were thankful for the faithful support of many individuals and families. It was a blessing to have some of those people gathered together to warmly greet us as we arrived home in Portland, Oregon. A Saturday in August is prime time for summer activities, and we appreciated the special effort that everyone made that evening to welcome

Wikelson and Richardson to their new home. And so we found our family and friends waiting just beyond the gate to greet us. Only Grace had traveled with us to lend a helping hand and so Emma, Daniel, and Anna were there at the gate waiting, and in a few minutes all eight members of the Garland family would be in one place at the same time. We were about to begin a new chapter—no, it was more than that. We were closing one book and beginning the next volume in the series that was our life together. Our family would never be the same again and that was a good thing. It was something that God had planned. He had asked us to step out in faith into his plan and He had been gracious enough to provide us with the faith to do so. It was a sweet, special, and surreal moment. It was a moment I had looked forward to for so long, and I was thankful that God had brought us faithfully there.

How can I explain the joy in a father's heart as Wikelson, seeing his brother and sisters waiting for him, walked confidently up to Daniel and gave him a warm embrace? Those two boys were very close in age, and I had been praying regularly that God would give them a special bond as brothers. While I knew that there would be conflict ahead, I was so pleased that their first interaction was literally picture perfect. In fact the entire greeting party was picture perfect, as the boys were welcomed into the arms of loving family and friends. There was no sense of fear or tears to be seen in Wikelson and Richardson. Only sweet smiles and innocent pride as they posed for pictures with all those new people. I am not sure how they wrapped their little minds around the concept, but they really seemed to understand that they were now a part of our family.

We all rode together on the shuttle bus to the economy parking lot where our car was waiting. At eight members strong, we easily filled up the back half of the shuttle—a feat that I was unsure whether to be proud of or scared about. Bus shelter "Blue N" was our stop, and we all piled out and headed for the car just a short distance away. Somehow we did not plan properly, and we actually had too many car seats. When you counted us and all of our stuff, we had no extra room for a bulky car seat and there were no volunteers to ride home with a large contraption in their lap, so we kind of hid the seat along the sidewalk where we had parked and drove away. Perhaps the next family who parked there would be one car seat short and they would find a pleasant surprise? Fortunately the seat that we donated to the economy parking lot was a last-minute pickup from a garage sale and cost around $10, so it wasn't a major loss. That was the first of many improvisations we would be making over the coming weeks in order to survive. Similar to leaving car seats in parking spaces, sometimes unorthodox practices are needed for a large family to function. I will not take the time to go into all the details here, but suffice it to say that there are times when "You have to do what you have to do!" We said our first prayer together as a family just before we headed out for home. We prayed for patience with each other and unity as a family, as well as thanking God for the opportunity He had given us to share His love with others.

The boys loved to ride in the "machin," but they loved even more the moment we pulled up to our house. The first few minutes home were as you would expect them to be as two little wide-eyed boys noisily explored, touched, opened, and experienced things they had never before seen except in pictures. The reality of being home was so much better than the pictures they had seen in the photo albums we made for them. Of course they had been very interested to see those two-dimensional images as we explained to them what their new life would look like, but, just like the adoption, those pictures were not an end in themselves—they pointed to something better. Remember that as wonderful as our adoption of Wikelson and Richardson was, it was an image of something even greater—that is, God's adoption of His children. The pictures the boys enjoyed seeing while they lived at the orphanage paled in comparison to exploring our home in person. Likewise our human adoption of them would one day pale in comparison to a full realization of our place in God's heavenly household as His redeemed and adopted children. I take nothing away from the value of the pictures we took to Haiti with us. They were among the most important pieces we carried as we traveled, because they pointed to what will be and we did not want the boys to miss out on that. It is interesting to note that those pictures were left behind at BRESMA having been either lost or destroyed and they were never missed at all. I would also take nothing away from the beauty and unique privilege of human adoption, but to deny that it pointed to a greater reality would be diminishing, not enhancing, its value. The act is precious not only because it is good in itself but also because of what it points to.

I could fill another book with stories about life with newly adopted children who came from a different country, culture, and language. Those first several months were crazy as we all learned to live with each other. One morning Emma, with a puzzled and disgusted tone asked, "Why is there a sock in the pancake mix?" That question is actually a very good indicator of what the adjustment period was like. I could not have summarized it better. After taking a week off to help the family adjust, I returned to a regular work schedule. Joelle was simply amazing in her ability to care for the needs of each child while still managing to start the homeschool year on time. Her one-room "schoolhouse" had just seen a 50 percent increase in student enrollment—and the new kids did not speak English. It is a marvel to me that she was able to keep everyone on task and moving forward in their education. To me it seemed like the ultimate cat-herding experiment, and I was thankful that she was up to the task—because I certainly was not.

Before this chapter closes, I want to share two of my favorite stories about our early days together. The first occurred on a warm summer afternoon, and Richardson was star of the show. All the younger kids (Emma, Daniel, Wikelson, and Richardson) were enjoying jumping on the trampoline, running through sprinklers, and soaking in a blue inflatable pool that in reality was much too small for any of them. I was sitting on the back patio, reclining in my favorite chair and sipping some homemade iced tea that had just the right amount of sweetness. I looked out across the yard, and my heart felt full and satisfied as I basked in the joy of laughter, fun, and bonding that I witnessed as all the kids played together. It was a perfect moment—a moment I had dreamt of many times as I sat in that same chair imagining the day when Wikelson and Richardson would at last be home. *This is what it is all about,* I thought as I gave myself the proverbial pat on the back. That is when it happened.

Richardson had finally mustered the courage to climb into the little pool with the other kids and was standing just behind Emma as she floated lazily on a small blow-up tube. I watched with a combination of shock and amusement as Richardson pulled down his pants to his ankles and proceeded to test how the pool would function as a toilet. He was extremely pleased with the high and arching stream he was able to produce as he watched it ripple and bubble into the clear water below. It took a moment for those in the pool to realize what was happening, but when they did, the reaction was something like the combination of stepping into an angry hornet's nest and a fire alarm going off. Emma, of course, was the most incensed, in part because she was the only female present and in part because she is the most sensitive member of our family when it comes to disgusting behavior. She ran from the pool with a look of sheer terror on her face and was only able to be consoled later when I explained to her that lots of kids pee in the public pool she enjoys swimming in, a revelation that added insult to injury but eventually seemed to calm her down. Meanwhile Richardson just kind of stood there with a "What's the big deal?" look on his face. It was an infraction on decency that was very hard to keep a straight face through as I comforted the wounded and helped to clean the yucky water out of the pool. Needless to say, everyone survived and one day will look back with laughter on that sunny afternoon.

The second story I will share is a story that Wikelson told me one evening as we were going through the bedtime routine. When we first met in November 2015, Wikelson had all of his teeth. That was no surprise because he had just turned five years old a few months earlier. When we returned for him in August, we noticed that three of his front teeth were missing. We already had some suspicion that perhaps Wikelson was one year older than his birth certificate claimed, and the rapid loss of teeth seemed to serve as more evidence that maybe he was six years old instead of five. But what he told me that evening cast some serious doubts on our theory. He was brushing his teeth after bath time. (I don't know how they did it, but whoever was in charge of teeth-brushing instruction at BRESMA was an absolute master teacher, because that kid could brush like a champ—and he enjoyed it!) He was on his second or third round of refilling his brush with toothpaste and working hard to clean the top front row. I was tidying up the bathroom, working just behind him where he stood on a small stool looking into the mirror.

He stopped brushing and, with a combination of physical acting, Creole, and English, began to tell his tale.

First he made a fist and acted out a punch to his face. Next he pretended to grab one of his teeth, and with a grunt he pulled as if to yank it from his jaw. Then he went through a series of what appeared to be old-school WWF wrestling moves complete with kicks, punches, and body slams. He continued to use one name over and over, making it clear that he and at least one other person were involved in the brawl. I questioned him on the story in several different ways, and I was able to gather that he had been in some sort of altercation at the orphanage and as a result had gotten three of his teeth knocked out! Once he was clear that I understood what he was saying, he smiled, and with a confident "Wi!" he returned to brushing his teeth. It was difficult to discern where the truthfulness of his tale merged with the imagination of a little boy trying to impress his new daddy and I had no way to verify any of the details. Nevertheless, the story remains a favorite for me, not because I endorse violence against my children, but just because of the way he told it and the fact that he seemed proud to tell it. I have no doubt that there were plenty of tears when and if it happened. I think I would cry too if I had three teeth knocked out. But that evening it was no more than a memory and I was glad that he wanted to share it with me.

CHILDREN DO NOT (ALWAYS) APPRECIATE ADOPTION

THERE IS A fairytale view of adoption where the perfect love of adoptive parents is reciprocated bountifully with an attitude of sweet thankfulness on the part of the adopted children. What child, after he had been rescued from a hopeless life of homelessness, would not freely and overwhelmingly reflect the love that had been shown to him by his parents? Wouldn't there be an almost obligatory appreciation for his new circumstances that would squelch any disobedience, rebellion, or complaining? Wouldn't he grow up to automatically adore and admire his parents and the sacrificial efforts they undertook to provide him with a home? Would it be reasonable for me to think that Wikelson and Richardson might be so pleased with their new home that they would forsake testing and trying behavior? Well, assuming that those boys are indeed human – the answer is no. It is human nature to forget where we came from and neglect the gracious sacrifices that have been made on our behalf. How do I know that is true? First of all, God's children demonstrated that forgetfulness beautifully in many of the Old Testament stories and if that were not enough, I see in myself a rather unfortunate, but excellent example of it as well.

After 400 years of living as slaves in the captivity of Egypt the Hebrew nation had just been miraculously rescued. They witnessed first-hand many spectacular miracles as God sent plague after plague down on the Egyptians. Those wonders culminated with the people walking across the Red Sea on dry land with the massive walls of water parted on either side. It was only three days after that great deliverance that the people began to grumble about a lack of water. It was not three months after leaving Egypt that they were saying, "Would that we had died by the hand of the Lord in the land of Egypt...for you have brought us out into this wilderness to kill this whole assembly with hunger" (Exodus 16:3). Despite His stubborn and unappreciative children, the Lord continued to provide for them causing bitter waters to turn sweet and raining down manna from heaven. Because of their lack of faith He eventually had to punish an entire generation making them wander in the wilderness for forty years before giving the Promised Land to their descendants. Through it all, God remained as a perfect example of a faithful and patient Father providing for His children. Can you imagine what you would do if you saw, among the other miracles, the Nile river turned to blood, locusts devastate the land, days of pitch black darkness, the death of all the first-born sons, the great pillars of fire and cloud guiding your escape, the parting of the Red Sea, the decimation of the Egyptian army, and the miraculous provision of food and water? I will give you a hint. Because you are a human being just like the Israelite people you would grumble in the wilderness and so would I. No matter how well I love my children, either biological or adopted, I know they will still rebel and grumble because that is what God's children did and continue to do.

I also know my children will grumble and misbehave because that is what I do. Words cannot describe the love that has been lavished upon my life by my Heavenly Father. It is simply beyond comprehension what God has done for me and all those who are willing to call on His name. When I was at my worst and entirely undeserving, at exactly the right time, Christ died for me. "For while we were still weak, at the right time Christ died for the ungodly. For one will scarcely die for a righteous person—though perhaps for a good person one would dare even to die— but God shows his love for us in that while we were still sinners, Christ died for us" (Romans 5:6-8). What if it is true that Jesus, who is God in the flesh, died the death that I deserved and paid all the debts that I owed causing me to stand righteous before the throne of God with no fear of condemnation? What if it is true that He has blessed me in Christ with every spiritual blessing in the heavenly places (Ephesians 1:3)? How would I act under those circumstances? Have I not been blessed more than the Israelites? They took God for granted after witnessing a series of earthly miracles. I forget His goodness even though He came to earth and died for me. Which is the greater blessing: deliverance from slavery in Egypt or God Himself giving His life for mine? Have I not been blessed many times more abundantly by God than Wikelson and Richardson have been blessed by me? Unfortunately, like all children, I do not always appreciate my Father. The fact is that I cannot really comprehend what has been done for me. My intellect can no more process an eternity without God than it can an eternity with God. I can fathom neither the riches and beauty that He has prepared for me nor the horror and darkness He has saved me from. I know that His goodness and love are beyond measure and yet I frequently stray from His arms. I often rebel, if not with my actions, then with my mind. The lure of lesser things draws my wandering eyes away from Him - my flesh falling for the lie that there could be something in this world that could satisfy me more. I am not proud to admit it, but my response to my heavenly Father has not always been a loving compliance with His will. I do not always trust the way I should and there are definitely occasions when grumbling overshadows gratefulness. As I seek to image God the Father for my children they might seek to image me as a son of the Father and so I need to be careful about the example I set. The way I respond to God as a child sets the tone for how they will respond to me.

Those boys have been taken from a very unfavorable situation and given as stable a home as I could provide them with. As I write these words, Haiti is just recovering from the most devastating hurricane to hit its shores in a decade. As if the poverty, disease, and loneliness were not enough, even the weather in their native country threatened their lives. In part because they cannot fully understand their circumstances and in part because they are like you and me as human beings they rebel, test boundaries, act ungrateful, and sometimes take for granted the blessings that they now enjoy. For example, how long do you think it would take a malnourished and chronically hungry child to develop picky eating habits once there is an abundance of food choices before him? Based on my experience the answer is about one week. Rather than holding these things against them I am convicted by them as I see my own lack of thankfulness for my Heavenly Father. How can I expect more of them than I expect of myself? Instead of condemning them I have sought to set an example for them. My hope is that as I demonstrate a heart of gratitude toward God they would model that heart in their own behavior. My desire is not only that they learn to honor me as their human father but also that they would be drawn to the goodness of God and one day place their hope in His unfailing love. As I relate to all my children I pray that God would impart to me a small portion of the patience He showed to the wandering Israelites so long ago and now shows to me daily. I am an imperfect Father and Anna, Grace, Emma, Wikelson, Daniel, and Richardson are imperfect children. May God's love bind us to one another and cover our weaknesses as we seek to put Him first.

A CALL TO FATHERS

WITHIN THE CHRISTIAN community the heart for adoption is all too often beating within the chests of women but not men. Orphaned children, it would seem, tug more at a mother's heartstrings, striking a resounding cord, while fathers remain silent or just follow along in an accompanying role. Because mothers tend to be more nurturing, it seems natural that they would lead the way when it comes to orphan care. Therefore Christian outreach through the ministry of adoption can be easily delegated to them because they seem to care the most about it. But isn't it interesting that in the Bible God chooses to describe orphans as the "fatherless" and never the "motherless"? There was something unique about the presence of a father in biblical times such that losing him would be devastating to the family unit, and the same thing holds true today. Losing fathers produces two groups of people:

orphans and widows. These are precisely the two groups that James called all Christians to care for as they live out their true religion: "Religion that is pure and undefiled before God the Father is this: to visit orphans and widows in their affliction, and to keep oneself unstained from the world" (James 1:27).

> *Christians should take special note of the fact that the Bible regularly pairs orphans and widows. The Bible also consistently uses the term "the father-less" as a synonym for "orphan." This is because in biblical times the large majority of orphans had lost their father but not their mother. This is the case today as well. An estimated 101 million of the 153 million children classified as orphans—more than six in ten—have a surviving mother.[5]*

When it comes to raising a child, a mother's role is vital and irreplaceable. I can say that with firsthand experience, because our children would be at a remarkable disadvantage if I was their sole parent. Joelle has a set of instincts in caring for little ones that I simply do not possess. For example, I sleep well at night when the kids have neglected to brush their teeth, but I am convinced that Joelle can actually feel the plaque building up on those little molars and she cannot rest until a thorough brushing has been

---

5 Christian Alliance for Orphans' White Paper: "On Understanding Orphan Statistics," accessed October 10, 2016, https://cafo.org/wp-content/uploads/2015/06/Christian-Alliance-for-Orphans-_On-Understanding-Orphan-Statistics_.pdf.

accomplished. Joelle meets needs in our home, even if it is not fun, popular, or comfortable for the kids she makes sure their little lives are in order from their teeth down to their toenails.

As important as a mother is, the loss of a father is devastating to the family unit. Whether it was the ancient land of Israel or the current nation of Haiti, a child who lost a father to war, disease, or abandonment often struggled to survive, even if the mother was still present. Due to extreme poverty—the likes of which we who live in the wealthiest country the world has ever known cannot comprehend—a single-parent family is often not viable. The mothers who are left suffer terribly because they are often forced to make the unthinkable decision of which children to feed and which to leave hungry. Living in a nonviable family arrangement creates orphans, not only in cases where the child has lost both parents, but also in situations that result in a single parent being wholly unable to care for a child. That is why the international definition of an "orphan" includes two subcategories: the single orphan (one surviving parent) and the double orphan (no surviving parents).

Both fathers and mothers are critical to the raising of children. The absence of a father, however, especially when it takes place in a developing country, produces a set of circumstances that makes a mother's job exponentially more difficult. The opportunity for the survival of children is diminished because of the failure to meet the most basic of needs. While it would obviously be difficult for a single father to raise children as well, that situation is far less common. Even in the United States, where Third World type poverty is almost never seen, the loss of a father still has serious implications for a child. The National Center for Fathering cites six consequences for children growing up in fatherless homes: increased risk of poverty, substance abuse, emotional disorders, academic failure, crime, and teenage sexual activity.[6] These difficulties show that even if life-threatening poverty is unlikely, children raised without a father suffer greatly.

When it comes to caring for those whom the Bible calls "fatherless," should it be just mothers who are leading the way? After all, as we saw from the statistics, many "orphan" children already have a mother—it is the father who is missing! Children who are missing fathers need fathers to seek them out and bring them home—just as the heavenly Father sought me out and is in the process of bringing me home. It would appear that in order to address the needs of the fatherless, we will need fathers to step up. Time after time I have heard stories of a mother who would like to consider adoption and the most significant obstacle is not availability, space, or finances, but instead it is her husband. What if Christian men, seeking to model their heavenly Father, became the driving and leading force behind orphan care? What if, instead of being immoveable anchors at worst, or willing accomplices at best, fathers led

---

6 National Center for Fathering, "The Consequences of Fatherlessness," accessed October 10, 2016, http://www.fathers.com/statistics-and-research/the-consequences-of-fatherlessness/.

the way into the lives of little ones in need? Instead of being a wet blanket, what if fathers fanned into flames that desire to help the helpless—a desire that is so often present in a mother's soul?

To be clear, many men have sought out, loved, and sacrificed for orphans in need. I commend them for their strong work and I hope to follow the example set by so many who have gone before me. My own adoption story did not begin with me but with Joelle. She carefully broached the subject and then allowed God to work on my heart until I was ready. Now that I have had time to meditate on God's adoption of me and our adoption of Wikelson and Richardson, I am jealous of her. I wish I had been the one to ignite the spark that has now led to such a warming and loving fire within our family: the invitation of the fatherless to join us. I am so thankful, however, for her godly encouragement of me and the unconditional support of my final decision. In the same way that she nudged me to consider adopting, I want to nudge other men to consider it as well.

"DON'T HUG THE BEAM!"

We traveled to Haiti to get our boys in August 2016 right in the middle of the summer Olympic Games. That was interesting timing, because some years ago our pastor used an Olympics-inspired illustration in his message that impacted me deeply. Looking back, I can now see that his message became among the first seeds planted that would one day grow into our adoption story. As I walked into the service that morning, something was different about the stage. Boldly standing out amongst the musical instruments, speakers, chairs, and decorations was an official-size gymnastic balance beam. At sixteen feet long, four inches wide, and suspended four feet off the floor by supports at either end, that apparatus was difficult to miss and definitely out of place. The take home message that day was "Don't hug the beam!"

Pastor Alan Hlavka gave the sermon, and he began by reminding us of the talent, precision, and time it takes for a gymnast to develop the skill to dance, flip, and twist through a beautiful routine with nothing but a four-inch beam in front of her. After finishing the routine, usually with an acrobatic dismount of the beam, the competitor will turn toward the judges and lift her hands in the air briefly and then return to the sideline to wait for their response. Using the prop to emphasize his point, Pastor Alan analogized the balance beam performance to the Christian life. As believers in Christ, we are eternally secure in the salvation purchased for us on the cross; however, we have been given work to do. As new creations in Christ, the workmanship of God, we are made to participate in His kingdom work. At the completion of our lives, we will give an account to God for the way we lived, not to gain entrance into heaven—because that is based alone in our faith in Christ—but for the purpose of gaining or losing eternal rewards. After the routine of our life is complete and we dismount the metaphorical beam, we will raise our hands in the air and look to God for His commendation. On that day all believers hope to hear the words, "Well done, good and faithful servant."

At that point the illustration had worked and the message was amplified by it, but was it really necessary to set up the actual beam on the stage? Wouldn't the analogy work just as well with a detailed description rather than by going through all the trouble of obtaining and setting up an actual piece of equipment? That was when Pastor Alan did something I may never forget. He turned and walked up to the beam as it sat there four feet above the floor. As he described a life of little faith that involved no risk for Christ, he climbed onto the beam and wrapped his arms and legs tightly around it, holding fast with all the strength he had with a fearful look on his face as if he was suspended fifty feet above the ground. After a short time he "dismounted" and then, raising his hands in the air with a look of accomplishment in his eyes, turned to where the judges would sit as if he had just completed a gold medal performance. The audience laughed at the absurdity of it all, because they could imagine what would happen if an actual Olympic competitor hugged the beam and then with a triumphant wave looked expectantly to the judges for a good score.

The point was well made. Isn't it true that many Christians, particularly in the United States, cling to their lives as one would "hug the beam," not willing to sacrifice or take any risk for the sake of the Gospel? I felt convinced that day that this is not what the Christian life is supposed to look like. It was not what the earliest Christians did as they risked their very lives to claim Christ as their Savior. We are not called to safe living. Jesus said, "For whoever would save his life will lose it, but whoever loses his life for my sake and the gospel's will save it" (Mark 8:35). When I first heard that message, I did not know how my life would change as a result, but I knew that I did not want to hug the beam. As hard as it was for me, over time I slowly released my death grip on the beam of my life, determined to stand up and walk, and maybe jump, and maybe with the Lord's help, do a flip or two before my time here on earth was over. I knew that I would stumble and probably fall many times, but I also knew that, just as a talented gymnast was born to compete at the highest level and not to hug the beam, I was born of God to *do*, not just *believe* the Gospel message. An Olympic competitor would never dream of hugging the beam, and that was the mind-set that I wanted as I continued to grow in my faith. My call to fathers is to not "hug the beam," but to prayerfully consider the work that God has prepared for you. Whether it be by taking in a homeless little one or by participating in some other sacrifice that God has called you to, I would encourage you to live a life with a Gospel-driven missional purpose in mind.

Just because human adoption has biblical parallels, it does not mean that every Christian should adopt. As we examined earlier, there are plenty of biblical images portrayed in marriage and parenting, but not all believers are commanded to participate in those things. For example, many Christians live very effective lives for Christ having never married. It is not my purpose to make a case from Scripture for all Christians to adopt. We are all image bearers of God and that image can be demonstrated in many different ways. Our lives as believers should and will look different as we serve God with the talent, gifting, and calling that He provides.

I do not consider every father as called to adopt, but I would call every father to consider adopting. Just be available. Pray about it. Seek God on how He might want to use you as a father to help support the fatherless. Perhaps that means adopting, or perhaps it means supporting an adoptive family through prayer, respite care, or with financial assistance. One of the most significant barriers to potential adoptive parents is the overwhelming financial obligations involved. International adoptions are particularly expensive, and at times those costs represent an impenetrable wall that stands between orphans and parents. Our adoption expenses were aided in part through a grant from Show Hope, a foundation started by Mary Beth and Steven Curtis Chapman to financially assist orphans and their adoptive families. An individual working through Show Hope, whom we will likely never meet this side of heaven, sacrificed financially to aid us in the completion of our adoption. Each member of our family, including Wikelson and Richardson, will be eternally grateful for that sacrifice.

Adoption is not the only way to care for children in need. What about foster care? I live in the state of Oregon, and there is always a shortage of willing foster parents to meet the needs of waiting children. Fostering is a temporary measure where parents "stand in the gap" to provide a home for children who are usually facing difficult or unsafe situations with their biological families. Whether it be through domestic adoption, international adoption, fostering, or a supportive role, I challenge fathers to get involved.

My prayer for fathers and one of my motivations for writing this book is to encourage us to step out to the front lines in the battle for orphans. Let us not be one more barrier but instead an active advocate for the fatherless who are in need of a home. As we look to the example set by our heavenly Father, may God grant each one of us the courage to follow in His steps according to our calling.

A CALL TO THE FATHERLESS

PERHAPS AFTER READING this book you have found some common ground with Wikelson and Richardson. While most of you are not orphans in the sense of having lost one or both parents, some of you may still be spiritual orphans lacking the love and fellowship of the heavenly Father. Some of you may be like I was before I reached out and accepted the great gift of salvation that God offers to all people though His Son Jesus. If you fall into that category, I would encourage you to embrace and not reject the Father who has sacrificed beyond comprehension to freely offer you a place in His home. If the Christian Gospel (good news about Jesus) is true then it is the best news anyone could ever imagine. It is worth investigating if you are a skeptic – after all why wouldn't you want it to be true?

My personal reason for faith is based on two facts that

(although many have tried) I believe cannot be denied. The first is the fact that we live in a created universe proving that there is indeed a God. There is no other viable explanation for why we are here other than that God put us here. The second fact is that Jesus rose from the dead proving that He was who He said He was – God incarnate. It has been said that the Resurrection is the most verifiable historical event in the ancient world. There is simply no other explanation for the Christian movement other than the Resurrection of Jesus. Because there is a God and Jesus proved that He is that God everything He says is true – including the most wonderful news of the Gospel.

Jesus said, "For God so loved the world, that he gave his only Son, that whoever believes in him should not perish but have eternal life" (John 3:16). If you would like to know more about the amazing love of God please email me at the address provided at the conclusion of this book or find a Christian who lives out their faith and ask him or her. Whatever you do, take some time to consider what God has done for you – you have nothing to lose and everything to gain by doing so! Do not remain a spiritual orphan. The Father has come to take you home. Enter into His family with joy!

EPILOGUE
Adoption in All Its Fullness

I WOULD DESCRIBE OUR first few weeks at home together as "full." Few things, if any, were done halfway. It was a time of extremes for our family. The highs were high and the lows were low. Those days were full of everything. At any moment we could alternate between teary eyes full of happiness to teary eyes full of sadness. Our house was full of noise, activity, exploring, learning, and love. There were plenty of days full of discipline as each child, whether adopted or biological, tested the boundaries of our new life together. We endured fits that seemed to come out of nowhere and last longer than I thought possible, each one followed by a full sense of emotional cleansing and a restored relationship with Mama and Papa.

There were times full of fear and times full of comfort. The nights were full of cries for "daddy" due to fear, growing pains, sadness, and sometimes just because. Like most people, I prefer to sleep uninterrupted but God gave me an extra measure of compassion when those calls woke me at night. I was struck by the fact that my mere presence was usually enough to comfort them. There was nothing I needed to do other than be there and that reminded me of the profound importance of a father's love. Being with them in those wee morning hours turned into a source of joy for me as I had the privilege of providing them with something they previously lacked as well as giving me an opportunity to reflect on the comforting presence of my own heavenly Father.

The boys experienced full tummies. Mealtimes were particularly wild and full of motion, surprises, and messes. Those kids could really eat. Often times even little Richardson would enjoy two to three times the amount of food I could handle. New tastes were met at first with apprehension but later with a full approval. The fullness of disgust at the first glimpse of a chocolate chip cookie was overcome by the fullness of pleasure at the discovery of tasting that warm, doughy goodness. The fullness of joy at the first taste of a Rhodes roll with butter was rivaled only by the fullness of terror at the sight of our dog, or a small rubber lizard toy that must have appeared very real by the screaming and panic it caused.

Playtime was especially full. It was full of laughter, yelling, bouncing, fun, and fighting. There was rarely a dull moment when Emma, Daniel, Wikelson, Richardson, and Kavik the dog were all outside together!

Our schedules were full. There was not a full hour of relief between the time they woke like clockwork at 6:30 a.m. until the final lights out at 9:00 p.m., after which we were typically too worn out to do much but kind of sit and stare at the wall. It wasn't that Wikelson and Richardson had struggles every hour, but even the happy times meant work for Mom and Dad, whether it be refereeing playtime outside, working on a craft, cleaning up a meal, or just trying to keep up with regular household duties. It seemed that much of the day, our arms were full of little people. The boys did not like to be left alone, and many times one of them, in particular Richardson, wanted or needed to be held. Holding him required some careful attention, because you could never tell exactly when he would come at you with a face full of wet kisses. I previously described the "love cup" that each of our children has and the need for it to be filled often. During that early phase, no matter how fully we filled that love cup in one day, we found it empty again the next morning.

Joelle and I saw our stress levels rise to full capacity. There were never times of full regret or a desire to "send them back," but there were perhaps some thoughts that approached those extreme thresholds. Adoption is not an easy undertaking and we were coming to a more full understanding of that with each passing day. While our hearts were full with the wear and tear of the trials, they were also full of a God-given love for those children. Reading a book, pushing a swing, or taking a ride in the "machin" brought a smile to the faces of Wikelson and

Richardson that left no doubt they were indeed home. The times of love and bonding that occurred even over the simplest of tasks filled us with a reassurance that we were walking the path that God had planned for us.

Adoption leaves you with a full plate in many ways. From loving to crying, teaching, helping, and holding, it is a full-time job. As we first started, I found my emotions easily moving back and forth between a contented satisfaction in providing a home for Wikelson and Richardson to a sense of doubt as I wondered if we had made a mistake with the decision to adopt. Over time we grew together as a family, and I felt a strong determination to remain in the work that God had called us to. The times that I was able to stop thinking about myself helped me to refocus on what we were doing. I wrote earlier that by deciding to adopt, I was giving up a part of my selfish life. That was not just a theoretical statement. It was a reality, and the more I sought to live sacrificially, the better father I was becoming—not just to the adopted boys, but to all my children.

Adoption is not an easy undertaking. It was not easy for God the Father, and it will continue to challenge me daily. I look forward to seeing those challenges through to the end and following hard after God and the good work He has called me to as I continue in this father's story.

OTHER BOOKS BY
MICHAEL G. GARLAND

The Glasses We Wear:
Reflections on Christian Worldview

The Lifted Veil:
Viewing Your World in the Knowledge of Christ

Available for Kindle and paperback at Amazon.com

Contact

reflectgod@gmail.com
Michael G. Garland at Facebook.com

67656240R10125

Made in the USA
Lexington, KY
19 September 2017